Who Knew?

Inside the Complexity of
American Health Care

Who Knew?

Inside the Complexity of American Health Care

The Essential Guide for Board Members, Trustees, Investors, Entrepreneurs, Politicians, Companies Providing Health Care-Related Products and Services, and Provider and Payer Organization CEOs, COOs, CFOs, and CIOs, and Patients

By

Lynn Harold Vogel, PhD

A PRODUCTIVITY PRESS BOOK

Routledge/Productivity Press
711 Third Avenue New York, NY 10017, USA
2 Park Square, Milton Park, Abingdon, Oxon OX14 4RN, UK

© 2019 by Taylor & Francis Group, LLC
Routledge/Productivity Press is an imprint of Taylor & Francis Group, an Informa business

---

Library of Congress Cataloging-in-Publication Data

Names: Vogel, Lynn Harold, 1945- author.
Title: Who knew? : inside the complexity of American health care / Lynn H. Vogel.
Other titles: Inside the complexity of American health care
Description: Boca Raton : Taylor & Francis, 2019.
Identifiers: LCCN 2018032590 (print) | LCCN 2018034936 (ebook) | ISBN 9780429434426 (e-Book) | ISBN 9781138353022 (hardback : alk. paper)
Subjects: | MESH: Delivery of Health Care | Health Care Reform | Medical Informatics | Quality Improvement | Health Services Administration | Socioeconomic Factors | United States
Classification: LCC RA393 (ebook) | LCC RA393 (print) | NLM W 84 AA1 | DDC 362.1068--dc23
LC record available at https://lccn.loc.gov/2018032590

Visit the Taylor & Francis Web site at
http://www.taylorandfrancis.com

and the CRC Press Web site at
http://www.crcpress.com

Dedicated to my wife, Lynn Carter, whose support for this project was essential to its completion; and to our children, Joanna and Benjamin, in the hope that a deeper understanding of health care's unique attributes can help to foster better access, greater affordability, and more demonstrable quality for the health care services they might need.

Contents

List of Figures

List of Tables

Acknowledgments

People who have enjoyed long careers often attribute at least some of their success—and longevity—to a small number of individuals who at points along the way have been helpful and influential. My career is no exception. Of course, parents play an outsized role not only in setting boundaries, but in creating possibilities and instilling values. My father was a man of great faith and served as pastor in a number of churches over his lifetime; my mother was a teacher and a committed minister's wife. In her fifties, however, she became a stock broker, determined not to let stereotypes totally define traditional roles. My parents' guidance and support were constant and unwavering throughout their lifetimes.

In college I met Harold Richman, the resident head for my dorm and a social worker with a distinguished career as a White House Fellow, teacher, and later Dean of the School of Social Service Administration at The University of Chicago. Harold was a friend, mentor, and colleague who remained available for consultations and guidance throughout his life. My transition to information technology was sparked by an opportunity at The University of Chicago Hospitals to become the Director of Information Services. Ken Bloem, the Hospital's executive vice president, facilitated this process into what subsequently defined much of my career. As chair of the Department of Biomedical Informatics at Columbia University, Edward (Ted) Shortliffe, a pioneer in biomedical informatics, provided a supportive and welcoming academic environment when I was a hospital administrator committed both to operations and to teaching. Ivo Nelson, then CEO of Healthlink, introduced me into the world of consulting and taught me about the importance of treating every client as a customer and identifying clearly the value you can deliver as a consultant.

Others along the way, too numerous to mention, contributed to what became an exciting and challenging career in health care management, information technology, and academia.

Translating my career experiences into this book has been a challenge, but one that has kept me up-to-date on the health care industry since leaving full time employment in 2012 and entering the world of consulting. It has also reunited me with at least one former student and colleague, Richard Caputo, who graciously read and commented on not one but two drafts of the manuscript. His thoughtful observations and suggestions helped significantly in making the book what it is. But of course, the final draft that became the published work is my responsibility and mine alone.

Note regarding endnote links: Almost every endnote contains a URL link, and all URLs listed in the endnotes for each chapter have been verified as working at the time of publication. However, websites do change their structures from time to time, which may contribute to links not working. If a link fails, we recommend that you cut and paste the URL or any endnote content manually into a browser.

Author

Lynn Harold Vogel, **PhD**, **LCHIME**, has been involved in information technology (IT) and academic medicine in the health care industry for more than 35 years, and is a widely recognized expert and presenter on health care and IT.

Dr. Vogel has served as vice president and CIO at academic medical centers in Chicago, New York, and Houston. In addition, he has held faculty positions in departments of Biomedical Informatics, Management, and Bioinformatics and Computational Biology.

Dr. Vogel has been named one of Computerworld's Premier 100 IT Leaders, and while at University of Texas MD Anderson Cancer Center, Computerworld designated that organization as a Laureate, and awarded its prestigious 21st Century Achievement Award in Health Care. He has also been recognized as one of InformationWeek's Healthcare CIO 25, and Becker Hospital Review's list of "100 Hospital and Health System CIOs to Know."

Dr. Vogel previously was a member and Fellow of the Healthcare Information Management Systems Society (HIMSS), a Certified Healthcare CIO (CHCIO) and continues as a member of the American Medical Informatics Association (AMIA). He is a Life Fellow (LCHIME) of the College of Healthcare Information Management Executives (CHIME), where he was a charter member, and previously served as board member and board chair. Dr. Vogel currently serves on the board of Glytec, a company focusing on the development and implementation of FDA approved software for glycemic management. He has his own consulting firm, LH Vogel Consulting, LLC (www.lhvogelconsulting.com), is a founding member of Next Wave Health Advisors (http://www.huntzingergroup.com/nwha), which is affiliated with the Huntzinger Management Group (www.huntzingermanagementgroup.com).

Dr. Vogel's education at the bachelor's, master's, and doctoral level was completed at The University of Chicago.

Dr. Vogel can be reached through his consulting company website.

Chapter 1

Introduction to the Complexity of Health Care

> *I have to tell you, it's an unbelievable complex subject ... nobody knew that health care could be so complicated.*[1]

Health care is a complicated business. But few efforts have been made to understand why this is so. Instead, we have a "revolving door" of companies attempting to provide new products to America's health care industry; politicians who too often fall short in their efforts to improve health care access and affordability; provider organizations that struggle to maintain operating margins; patient outcomes that seem difficult to measure; data breaches that occur more frequently and with greater impact in health care than in other industries; and information technology investments that fail to change health care while at the same time doing so successfully in other industries. And in general, as an industry, health care seems much more resistant to change than almost every other industry.

   This brief series of essays is intended increase the reader's understanding of how health care organizations work and the factors that make health care arguably the most complex industry in the American economy. In addition, each essay documents the fact that while information technology (IT) investments have made a dramatic impact in most industries, in health care they seem to have been decidedly less so.

The discussion that follows is especially relevant for companies working in health care, for provider organizations seeking ever more efficient and effective services, for government officials and politicians proposing new policies or programs or changes to existing health care policies and programs, for trustees and board members overseeing health care organizations, and, in the end, for the patients who depend on all of these for understanding whatever illnesses they might have and for increasing the likelihood of success in treating those illnesses.

How often is the point made in both formal and informal settings that "health care lags behind other industries in its investment in information technology"? Unfortunately, in the discussions about the challenges facing health care policy and practice, high-level generalizations about cause and impact confuse specific issues that in their own way need to be better understood. And again, the complexity of the industry itself creates barriers to the successful use of information technology.

Many in the business community think that the health care "business" is like every other industry, and that if only "business practices" could be applied to health care, hospitals would work much better. But there is much about health care that is unique. Jeff Goldsmith, a frequent commentator on health care issues, has observed:

> Health care services are not only the prototypical knowledge business, but also are perhaps the most complex product of our economy. More variability and uncertainty at the point of service exists in health care than in any other service in our economy.[2]

With such "variability and uncertainty" in the health care business, it should not be surprising that, for example, measuring patient outcomes consistently is difficult, or that patients often fail to understand their own health care issues, or that IT solutions may not work especially well.

Goldsmith's comment echoes observations made initially by Peter Drucker, who famously stated:

> The best example is the hospital—altogether the most complex human organization ever devised, but also, in the past 30–40 years, one of the fastest-growing types of organizations in all developed countries.[3]

By extension, if hospitals themselves are complex, it is fair to assume that that the health systems into which an increasing number of hospitals large and small are being organized, add even more complexity. Combining many individually complex organizations into an even larger organization only increases the level of complexity as layers and interrelationships are added to what is already an individually complex organization.

Asserting that an activity or set of activities is "complex" often sounds more like a defensive statement than an observation with some level of objectivity. However, a compelling argument can be made in support of Drucker's assertion by examining more closely the factors that contribute to complexity in health care.[4]

Over the past 20 years, numerous companies have failed in their efforts to provide successful, sustainable IT products to the health care industry. The list in some ways reads like a "who's who" of large and otherwise successful IT companies. Some examples:

1. IBM – one of the pioneers with their Patient Care System (PCS) in the late 1960s and early 1970s, but later sold much of the business to Baxter.

2. Unisys – had one of the early integrated registration and billing systems, as well as very sophisticated mainframe hardware architecture, but ended up abandoning both.
3. Hewlett Packard (HP) – was at one time a leading maker of monitoring equipment but left the business.
4. Baxter – acquired software assets from IBM and worked in partnership with IBM but subsequently left the business.
5. Siemens – acquired Shared Medical Systems (SMS), then attempted a re-write of their core software products and ended up selling their health care application business to Cerner, which is slowly sunsetting the Siemens/SMS products.
6. Microsoft – on several occasions has made significant commitments to the health care industry only to abandon them or sell them to other companies.
7. Google – made a significant investment in Google Health only to abandon the product several years after introduction.

It should be noted that IBM, Apple, Google, and Microsoft have all returned to the health care industry after historically entering and leaving at various times. The size of the industry appears to be irresistible even with a history of less than successful efforts. As large, technologically driven companies, their focus is typically on how to adapt their technologies to the health care industry rather than looking at what specific technologies the industry needs to improve. For Google and IBM, their investments in artificial intelligence are their primary mode of entry. For Apple, the focus is on leveraging the iPhone capabilities. Microsoft's efforts attempt to leverage existing and developing product suites for the health care market. However, these approaches have had limited success in the past, in part because of the challenges facing strategies that attempt to introduce expensive technologies into an industry that is beset by unconnected silos of data, ambiguity of terminology, continually declining payment models and consumers who simply lack trust in the abilities of large technology companies to protect and secure their medical data.[5]

Over the past several years, there have been no lack of "start-ups" in health care, as entrepreneurs seek to capitalize on the vast sums of money spent each year on health care products and services. In 2016 over $3 trillion was spent for health care in the United States—a vast sum by any standard.[6] And many companies assume that gaining access to even a small portion of those expenditures could drive a profitable business. During the first half of 2015, for example, more than 136 digital health start-ups received over $2 billion in funding.[7]

Unfortunately, many health care start-ups fail to survive— by one count 98% fail—and one primary reason is that "the founders of such companies don't pay enough mind to health care's idiosyncrasies."[8] Some of these include:

1. The complexity of the health care industry itself, in which common business models from other industries simply do not work well
2. A lack of understanding of the role that physicians play as "front line" workers in an industry in which these workers historically have not worked for the provider organization
3. Not realizing the limitations of patients as customers who don't pay the full cost of the services they receive and often have limited knowledge of the quality of the services being provided
4. Assuming that return on investment models used in typical business settings will apply in a straightforward fashion to IT investment decisions being made in health care
5. The sweeping changes taking place in health care with the increasing focus on "personalized" medicine and, relatedly, the role that genomics is playing in decisions about health care diagnosis and treatment

Health care is unique in that not only are specific components of the industry complex, but how they interrelate is complex as well. This leads to what we might call "systemic complexity"—complex parts interacting in complex ways to create an overwhelmingly complex industry.

Other industries have complex components, but none appear to have the overall "systemic complexity" that health care exhibits. The manufacture of automobiles, for example, is certainly a complex set of inter-related processes, but distribution and selling are relatively straightforward. Similarly, the insurance industry has complex components such as actuarily based premium calculations, but again the selling and purchase of insurance is quite straightforward. Even in the financial services industry, products such as credit default swaps are complex in themselves, but don't make the entire industry complex at the level that health care complexity approaches.

Components that create a "systemic complexity" combine to make an industry difficult to enter with new products and services, difficult to find appropriate levers to manage costs and a challenge for measuring the quality of the services being provided.

Most industries offer products and services to virtually anyone who can pay. In health care, access is limited by providers and payers engaged in a complex payment system in which customers (i.e., the patients) seldom pay a significant portion of the costs of the services they receive. Determining the quality of what is provided is also more difficult in health care than in industries in which the quality of services and products can be measured more readily.

Investment returns from health care start-ups in general have been poor. Expectations about developing new applications that will "disrupt" the industry have typically fallen short. The overall number of provider organizations is shrinking, leaving a smaller number of very large hospital and health systems, which because of their size and complexity, are slow to adapt. The federal government is the largest payer for services, which also means that payments for services are overseen by a huge bureaucracy—another built-in factor that must be considered when proposing any major changes. As one entrepreneur noted:

> There are many reasons for start-up failures, but most boil down to "health care is different." It's highly regulated, which makes rapid transformation difficult. The incumbents are massive enterprises with multiple services, so challenging them is nearly impossible. It isn't a market-driven industry that responds to better, cheaper, faster. … All the incentives are misaligned.[9]

Throughout this book, the author examines the major factors leading to health care's complexity and documents the contribution that each makes, which has resulted in an industry that has continuously frustrated improvement efforts by health care policy makers, provider organization managers, payers, clinicians, and patients.

- Chapter 1 provides an introduction to the complexity of health care.
- Chapter 2 discusses how health care, as a "services-based" business, differs in important ways from a "product-based" business model, the basis for many business "best practices."
- Chapter 3 examines the unique role that physicians play in the health care industry (which doesn't seem to be replicated in other large industries) and who are probably the most highly educated (and often most highly compensated) front line workers in any industry.
- Chapter 4 identifies the challenges of working with patients who often don't understand their own health challenges.
- Chapter 5 reviews the challenges of measuring the Return on Investment and the quality of the services that are provided in the health care industry.

- Chapter 6 explores the increasing complexity in the field of medicine more generally (especially with the onset of genomic medicine).
- Chapter 7 reviews the challenges that come from having patient data created and stored in multiple formats and systems.
- Chapter 8 discusses the special challenges presented by privacy and security challenges that apply specifically to the health care industry.
- Chapter 9 examines the political side of health care, discussing both the politics of health care generally and the politics that occur inside provider organizations.
- Chapter 10 examines how markets work (or in many cases, do not) in the health care industry, especially with much of the payment for health care services coming from third parties who are not directly involved in the buyer/seller transaction.
- Chapter 11 presents concluding observations.

The author has had a distinctive career as an "insider," with deep knowledge of the challenges of improving health care access and quality and of the special issues surrounding information technology investments. Companies and provider organizations, politicians, and policy makers and board members alike can benefit from leveraging the author's experience and knowledge to improve the opportunities for continuously enhancing the quality of care provided as well as the productivity of relationships between vendors and provider and payer organizations, which should over time work for the benefit of the patients.

Notes

1. President Donald Trump, televised press conference, February 27, 2017. https://www.youtube.com/watch?v=NXFr6_cJJTc. (Accessed on June 19, 2018.)

2. See the extended discussion by Goldsmith, J., "How Will the Internet Change Our Health System?" *Health Affairs*, January-February 2000, 9, 148. See https://www.healthaffairs.org/doi/pdf/10.1377/hlthaff.19.1.148. (Accessed on June 19, 2018.)

3. Peter Drucker, "They're not Employees, They're People," *Harvard Business Review*, February 2002, 74. See https://hbr.org/2002/02/theyre-not-employees-theyre-people. (Accessed on June 19, 2018.)

4. For an excellent discussion of "complexity," with health care examples, see Thomas G. Kannampallil, et al., "Considering Complexity in Healthcare Systems," *Journal of Biomedical Informatics*, December 2011, 44(6):943-7. https://www.science-direct.com/science/article/pii/S1532046411001067?via%3Dihub. (Accessed on June 19, 2018.) See also Craig Kuziemsky, "Decision-making in Healthcare as a Complex Adaptive System," *Healthcare Management Forum*, 2016, 29(1) 4–7. Also, Kon Shing Kenneth Chung, "Understanding Decision Making through Complexity in Professional Networks," *Advances in Decision Sciences*, Volume 2014, Article ID 215218. https://www.hindawi.com/journals/ads/2014/215218/. (Accessed on June 19, 2018.)

5. For more information regarding Apple's efforts, see http://www.healthcareitnews.com/news/apple-reveals-39-hospitals-launch-apple-health-records. (Accessed on June 19, 2018.) For Google, see http://www.modernhealthcare.com/article/20180419/NEWS/180419911. (Accessed on June 19, 2018.) For IBM's Watson initiative, see http://www.mobihealthnews.com/content/ibm-shares-data-how-watson-augments-cancer-treatment-decision-making. (Accessed on June 19, 2018.) For Microsoft, see https://www.zdnet.com/article/microsoft-tries-again-to-tackle-healthcare-with-new-services-tools/, and Tom Warren, "Microsoft Health Is a New Effort to Push Doctors to the Cloud," *The Verge*, June 27, 2018, https://www.theverge.com/2018/6/27/17509096/microsoft-healthcare-cloud-systems. (Accessed on June 19, 2018.)

6. National Health Expenditure Fact Sheet 2016. https://www.cms.gov/research-statistics-data-and-systems/statistics-trends-and-reports/nationalhealthexpenddata/nhe-fact-sheet.html. (Accessed on June 19, 2018.)

7. See, for example, the Digital Health Funding 2015 Midyear Report by @Rock Health. https://rockhealth.com/reports/digital-health-2015-midyear/. (Accessed on June 19, 2018.)

8. See, for example, Becker's Health Care IT and CIO Report, "98% of Digital Health Startups Fail—Here's Why," May 18, 2016. http://www.beckershospitalreview.com/healthcare-information-technology/98-of-digital-health-startups-fail-here-s-why.html. (Accessed on June 19, 2018.)

9. Thomas Goetz, "I Tried to Revolutionize Health Care. Here's Why It's So Hard to Crack." *Inc.* May 26, 2017. https://www.inc.com/magazine/201706/thomas-goetz/healthcare-disruption-never-happened.html. (Accessed on June 19, 2018.)

Chapter 2

Health Care Services: Difficult to Define, Difficult to Measure

2.1 Introduction

Service-providing jobs have been increasing dramatically over the past 40 years and currently represent about 80% of all jobs in the U.S. economy. Over just the past two decades this increase has accelerated. Consider the following statistics: in 1990, manufacturing employed more workers than any other sector in 36 states; by 2014, manufacturing was the major employer in only seven states. During the same time period, health care and social assistance industries nearly doubled in size, from 9.1 million in 1990 to just over 18 million in 2014, and became the largest employers in 34 states.[1]

What is ironic about these changes is that our ability to evaluate the quality of services in general has not kept pace with their role in our economy. The debate over how to measure the quality of services provided in both health care and education, for example, has gone on for years and is nowhere close to being resolved.

In health care, advances have been made in understanding the origins of many diseases and how to treat them, but the fact remains that we still know too little about either origins or effectiveness.[2] The Patient Protection and Affordable Care Act[3] (ACA) laid formal ground work to enable Medicare reimbursement processes to shift from paying clinicians for specific services performed to paying for overall performance (i.e., quality). This shift has been called the change from "paying for volume" to "paying for value," since previously payments for health care services were based primarily on specific visits or procedures performed and not on what happened as a result of those visits or procedures.

The passage of the ACA legislation did not solve one of the fundamental challenges in health care: measuring the value of health care services. Even after years of effort, there is still almost no agreement on the appropriate standards for measuring either the quality or the efficiency of care given to patients. The Agency for Healthcare Research and Quality (AHRQ) has identified more than 2,200 metrics promulgated by more than 100 separate organizations, leading to measurements that are poorly coordinated, lack consistency and often duplicate both measurement and reporting activities.[4]

This has a particular impact on companies offering information technology (IT) products to the health care industry. They are clearly entering uncharted territory. At the very least, a company would like to be able to demonstrate that the IT products they are providing to the health care industry are a good investment for their customers. But, if the services themselves have outcomes that are difficult to measure, it is even more difficult for companies providing IT products to demonstrate the effectiveness of what they are selling.

There is no question that in terms of revenue, profits, and losses, health care functions like a "business." But many companies mistakenly assume that as a business, health care must function like other businesses and operate on the same principles of value creation that non-health care businesses use. Interestingly, the nature of the business model followed by companies offering *products* to the health care industry is different from the business model followed in health care, which is based on *services*.

2.2 Measuring the Impact of Services versus Products

In any service encounter there is a service provider and a service receiver. In the case of health care, the provider is the *clinician* (typically a physician), and the receiver is the *patient*. But how does the patient know whether the product s/he is buying or the service s/he is receiving is in fact providing the value that was expected? While both products and services are involved in many health care transactions, for the most part health care consumers view that what they are receiving is a service—a transaction designed to lead from an unacceptable or unwanted level of health to a higher or better level.[5]

Evaluating whether a specific "service" is "worth it" brings a level of complexity to the transaction that is usually greater than determining whether a product that has been purchased is "worth it." Products are tangible items, something that can typically be touched, examined at length, viewed against alternatives and perhaps even used on a trial basis before reaching a final verdict as to whether it has a value commensurate with the payment that is expected. When one purchases a product, whether it is a car, an appliance, food or clothing, it is generally assumed that within a short period of time, the value of that purchase can be determined quite clearly. Not so with many services, and particularly services provided in the health care industry where the determination of value (e.g., becoming less ill or experiencing a complete cure) may take months or years.

Other major differentiators between products and services include:

Products are owned while services are delivered: When a product is delivered, the "ownership" of the product changes hands whereas with a service the "ownership" remains with the person providing the service. A physician providing a cancer diagnosis to one patient has not in any sense given up ownership of that diagnosis since in this case (and any other case in which a clinician is providing a service) there is no sense of ownership of a diagnosis or anything else related to the transaction.

Homogeneity of products versus heterogeneity of services: Products are considered homogeneous in the sense that they are created according to standards that define what the product should be. While there may be variations in the same type of product coming from the same production process, manufacturers do strive as much as possible to produce the same product each time. Services, on the other hand, vary with each act of delivery due in large measure to the fact that the service itself is defined by the specific interaction that takes place between the provider and the receiver of the service. In health care, for example, the service that the physician delivers to the patient at a specific time and place, even if it carries a similar title (e.g., an internist performing a history and physical with a patient), can differ because different physicians providing this service to different patients effectively results in a different transaction each time. In fact, for the most part, we want products to be well defined before we acquire them but want our services to be tailored each time to our individual needs and requirements.

Products exist past the acquisition process whereas services exist only as they are delivered: We expect products such as cars, vacuum cleaners and DVDs to exist and provide value long after we have acquired them.

Services, however, for the most part cease after the transaction is completed. Once a patient has had a visit with a physician, for example, that visit occupies a unique and time-limited place in the lives of both the patient and physician and cannot be repeated, and no longer exists past the point at which the transaction itself ends. The effects of the service may extend past the transaction, but the service itself ends.

The point of these rather commonsensical contrasts is to emphasize that any comparison between services and products must acknowledge that any service is by its nature more transitory and more complex than just about any product, and in health care, the effectiveness of the services being provided is often not clear until weeks or months later.

2.3 Measuring the Quality of Services

Companies providing products to the health care industry for the most part expect their products to enhance the quality of the service being provided.[6] But the quality of the service is often "in the eye of the beholder" and difficult to measure—how does a patient determine whether the clinical service and any associated products they may have received are "good" or not? And determining the cost of a service transaction is far more difficult than determining the cost of a product being sold, due to the unique characteristics of "service" indicated above. Therefore, company claims about their product(s) "enhancing the quality of a service" need to be aware of the challenges and subtleties of making these claims in an industry in which services are the driving force and subject to wide variation. There are no simple business models to make these determinations in the health care industry.

Public and private organizations have struggled to measure the outcomes of the services provided in the health care industry. Most common perhaps is the Healthcare Effectiveness Data and Information Set (HEDIS), developed by the National Committee for Quality Assurance. The HEDIS contains over 80 "clinically specific" measures that, combined with cost data, are often used to identify both high and low performing providers.[7] Other organizations often have different sets of service quality measures. The Center for Medicare and Medicaid Services, for example, defines over 1,500 different measures across 22 programs, with some measures applicable to some providers and not to others.[8]

Professional associations often develop their own measures of quality:

The Global Initiative for Chronic Obstructive Lung Disease has identified a set of outcomes and process aims for managing Chronic Obstructive Pulmonary Disease (COPD).[9]

The American Heart Association publishes guidelines for 14 cardiovascular conditions, including stroke, heart failure and acute myocardial infarction.[10]

The American Diabetes Association sets targets for glucose levels while patients are hospitalized.[11]

The Institute for Clinical Systems Improvement issues recommendations and protocols in 12 clinical areas, including palliative care, patient safety and reliability, and behavioral health.[12]

The Infectious Diseases Society of America sets standards for what antimicrobials should be used and how frequently they should be given in different situations.[13]

The Joint Commission on Hospitals and Health Systems (the health industry's primary accrediting agency) in general aligns its measures for health failure and acute myocardial infarction with those of the federal government's Centers for Medicare and Medicaid Services (CMS)—an important step forward—but Commission also has 12 other measure sets.[14]

Efforts to measure quality in health care can be quite burdensome. A recent study found that on an annual basis across four common specialties, an individual physician can spend 785 hours per year reporting on quality measures, resulting in an overall annual cost of more than $15.4 billion across the industry.[15]

In general, quality measures for health care services focus more on processes than on specific outcomes.[16] In part this is due to the fact that measuring processes in health care (e.g., how many patients received flu shots, how many days the patient was in the hospital, whether the nurse followed specific procedures when administering an injection, etc.) is much easier that measuring outcomes (e.g., whether the flu shot actually prevented the patient from getting the flu, or whether the patient actually got better from being in the hospital, or whether the injection was actually beneficial to the patient). In short, it is easier to determine whether a clinician followed a specific protocol than whether the protocol resulted in the patient getting better.

Perhaps the most ambitious effort to date to measure the quality of health care services has been undertaken by the AHRQ and its National Quality Measures Clearinghouse (NQMC), designed to stimulate and catalogue measures of evidence-based quality.[17] These measures are organized into five specific domains: Access, Outcome, Patient Experience, Process and Structure across five different settings: Ambulatory Procedure/Imaging Center, Ambulatory/Office-based Care, Community Health Care, Hospital Inpatient and Hospital Outpatient. At this point there are over 240 measures focused specifically on patient outcomes and a total of more than 1,900 measures related to all five clinical quality categories. This effort highlights again the complexity not only of measuring the quality of services but the extraordinary challenges facing service quality measurement in health care.

Figure 2.1 illustrates the extent of the problem: measures listed as "outcomes" are much more likely to focus on "processes" than actual patient outcomes.[18]

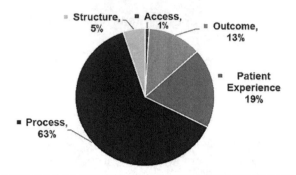

Figure 2.1   Percentage distribution of categories of quality measures (N = 2232). (Data from National Quality Measures Clearinghouse of the Agency for Healthcare Research and Quality [AHRQ].)

Many quality initiatives in health care rely on process metrics pioneered outside of health care; these include Six Sigma, Kaizen, TQM, and Lean, among others. With an historical focus on getting paid for services by documenting specific events and submitting claims to third parties, health care has been preoccupied with measuring the processes of delivering care. Most patients, however, are more interested in outcomes than in participating in the most efficient processes—they may complain about how much time is spent waiting to see the doctor, but if the results are good, the wait will likely be seen as "worth it."[19]

In Figure 2.2, the "Process" measures are further broken down by type.[20] The "Functional Status of Patient" measure reflects measurement taken at a point in time, usually either as a percentage of patients having X condition or scoring a specific value on some type of standardized measurement instrument. Few measurements appear to be linked to the outcome of a particular procedure or intervention.

One of the major challenges of collecting quality measures is establishing a connection between interventions and outcomes. How do we determine whether a particular intervention was the reason that a particular patient outcome was achieved? In some cases, patients improve on their own; in others, extraneous factors may be present that facilitate a positive outcome quite independent of a specific intervention.

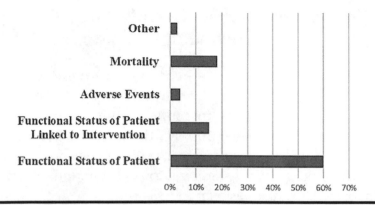

Figure 2.2   Percentage distribution of types of outcomes measures (N = 280). (Data from National Quality Measures Clearinghouse of the Agency for Healthcare Research and Quality [AHRQ].)

Figures 2.1 and 2.2 indicate that measurements of quality cover a range of activities, and only a relatively small percentage focus explicitly on outcomes. In addition, only 28% of the outcome measures in the National Quality Measures Clearinghouse of the AHRQ have been endorsed by the National Quality Forum (NQF), a nonprofit organization established to validate measures of quality in health care:

> NQF is the only consensus-based health care organization in the nation as defined by the Office of Management and Budget. This status allows the federal government to rely on NQF-defined measures or health care practices as the best, evidence-based approaches to improving care. The federal government, states, and private-sector organizations use NQF's endorsed measures, which must meet rigorous criteria, to evaluate performance and share information with patients and their families.[21]

This underscores the observation that measuring the quality of health care services continues to be a significant challenge and contributes substantially to the overall complexity of the health care industry.

2.4 Improving Services Quality through Information Technology

Historically companies have sought to improve the products and services they offer through investments in information technology. With these investments, they have sought to reduce their labor costs, improve the productivity of their workers, and offer new services or products not possible in the absence of IT. (We discuss this process more thoroughly in Chapter 5). Companies' experience with IT investments has not always delivered the results they expected. In fact, cost overruns, challenges in identifying specific benefits and outright failures seem to be more the rule than the exception. IT investments to improve the quality of services have been particularly challenging. As we noted earlier, defining appropriate measures of services quality have been particularly problematic and as a fallback, the focus becomes improving the processes of providing services, not the services themselves.

With the 1991 publication of The Institute of Medicine's *The Computer-Based Patient Record: An Essential Technology for Health Care* the claim that information technology, and electronic patient records in particular, could improve patient outcomes was a stimulus for initiating a major shift in IT investments in health care.[22] Although improving clinical workflows was a clear objective, improving the outcomes of those workflows was also of great importance.

In 1999, the Institute of Medicine published *To Err is Human,*[23] an exhaustive review of the challenges inherent in reducing medication errors that resulted in the deaths of close to 100,000 patients each year. Rather that attempting to affix blame to individuals, however, the report focused on the "safety of care" as

> a property of a system of care, whether a hospital, primary care clinic, nursing home, retail pharmacy or home care, in which specific attention is given to

ensuring that well-designed processes of care prevent, recognize, and quickly recover from errors so
that patients are not harmed.[24]

In the space of a few short years, the argument for the
introduction of electronic medical records was tempered by
the recognition that the challenge of improving the quality
of health services (in this case, the reduction of medication
errors) would require significant changes beyond just the introduction of computers.

Figure 2.3 depicts the successive investment themes in
health care IT over the forty-year period prior to the beginning of the 21st century. Virtually all these investments were
focused on improvements in processes—billing processes, laboratory and pharmacy processes, materials management, logis-
tics, clinical workflow, etc. The major exception was for the
investment in cost accounting systems, which were intended
to capture all the various cost components that comprised a
specific health care service. Interestingly, these systems represented some of the more complex investments at that time.
Improvements in the value proposition for health care IT
investments targeted at process improvements are challenging
on their own, but it is unclear whether these investments had
any significant impact on patient outcomes.

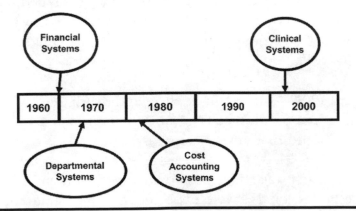

Figure 2.3 Progression of health care IT investments.

The challenges of improving the quality of services through IT investment have become apparent since the initial discussions in the 1990s. Electronic medical records (EMR) capabilities since then have focused almost exclusively on improving the processes of collecting, managing and accessing patient data without clear evidence that the outcomes of these processes have changed significantly.[25] And while one might argue that with more patient data readily available, better outcomes must surely follow, it is not yet clear that these process improvements truly lead to better patient outcomes.

Investments in EMRs continued slowly during the early 2000s, until the passage of The American Recovery and Reinvestment Act of 2009 (ARRA)[26] which contained specific incentives for health care provider organizations and professionals to use electronic medical record systems.

2.5 "Meaningful Use" of Health Care IT

Beginning in January 2011, the federal government developed metrics to stimulate EMR acquisition and implementation—and actual use—through a series of measures designed to capture "meaningful use." But again, recognizing the challenges of measuring the value of the services which EMRs were expected to enhance, Meaningful Use measures relied more on process improvements than improvements in outcomes. Meaningful Use requirements were to be implemented in three stages[27]:

Stage 1 (2011–2012): Data Capture and Sharing
Stage 2 (2014): Advance Clinical Processes
Stage 3 (2016): Improve Outcomes

Within each stage, Eligible Provider organizations and Eligible Professionals[28] were expected to demonstrate their compliance with a series of measures in order to receive incentive funds from the federal government. Measures in the first two stages were focused on process improvements; in the third stage, there was an expectation that by demonstrating the "meaningful use" of EMRs, patient outcomes would be improved.

In October 2015, the final rules for Stage 3 Improve Outcomes from the Meaningful Use measures were released with their expected focus on improving patient outcomes. Objectives and measures Eligible Professionals and Eligible Providers focused on:

1. Protecting electronic protected health information (ePHI)
2. Generating and transmitting permissible prescriptions electronically (eRx)
3. Implementing clinical decision support (CDS) interventions focused on improving performance on high-priority health conditions
4. Using computerized provider order entry (CPOE) for medication, laboratory, and diagnostic imaging orders
5. Providing patients (or a patient-authorized representative) with timely electronic access to their health information and patient-specific education
6. Engaging with patients or their authorized representatives about the patient's care
7. Providing a summary of care record when transitioning or referring their patient to another setting of care
8. Actively engaging with a public health agency or clinical data registry to submit electronic public health data in a meaningful way[29]

Even with an explicit effort to arrive at Meaningful Use measures focusing on Improving Outcomes, a cursory review indicates that measuring the *outcomes* of EMR use remains problematic. Processes of service delivery are still paramount whereas judgments about the results of those processes are for the most part still missing. Again, this is because measuring the value of services, even with IT investments designed to enhance the value of those services, continues to elude us.

As good as the intentions were for the Health Information Technology for Economic Clinical Health Act (HITECH), the judgments about its success in attaining its goals are not consistently positive. At best, the goals of cost reduction, improvements in care quality and greater efficiency are still inconclusive.[30]

In general, without adequate and accepted measures of quality, it is very difficult to make judgments about whether EMRs as currently implemented are actually being "meaningfully used."

Introducing electronic computing capabilities into any industry is difficult under the best of circumstances. When that industry is composed almost exclusively of services and not the production of physical products, the challenges are much greater. IT investments can improve the process of providing services, for example, by making historical data more available at the point of service and by creating large repositories based on the collection of data from numerous service transactions. But translating all of this data into actual improvements in each service as it is offered, particularly given the inherent the diversity of services offered in health care, is a unique challenge. The delivery of services, combined with other factors discussed in subsequent chapters, drives the complexity of the health care services environment beyond what we see in any other industry and makes IT investments all the more challenging.

Notes

1. Reid Wilson, "Watch the U.S. Transition from a Manufacturing Economy to a Service Economy, in One GIF," *The Washington Post*, September 3, 2014. https://www.washingtonpost.com/blogs/govbeat/wp/2014/09/03/

watch-the-u-s-transition-from-a-manufacturing-economy-to-a-service-economy-in-one-gif/?utm_term=.f7ad4044db71 . (Accessed on June 13, 2018.)

2. A similar situation prevails in education as demonstrated by the ongoing debate over the Common Core initiative.

3. This Act (which became known as the Affordable Care Act or "Obamacare") was signed into law by President Obama in March 2010 and represented perhaps the most sweeping health care reforms since the passage of Medicare and Medicaid legislation in 1965. For a detailed look at the Affordable Care Act, see https://www.healthcare.gov/glossary/patient-protection-and-affordable-care-act/. (Accessed on June 13, 2018.)

4. For more discussion, see "What Does Good Medicine Look Like?" *Bloomberg Business Week*, May 11, 2015, pp. 30–31.

5. The products involved in supporting a clinical service transaction, such as medicines that are prescribed, are provided in the context of a service delivered by a clinician. So, in the cases in which a health care consumer receives some type of product, it is usually the diagnostic skills of the clinician that lead to product recommendation and not a specific choice by the consumer. However, it should be noted that the extensive media coverage of medicines available only by prescription may lead some patients to request specific products from their physician.

6. Alternatively, companies may argue that their products result in lower service costs, which can in many cases be measured more directly than improvements in service quality.

7. Jared Capo, "Why We Need to Shift Healthcare Quality Measures from Volume to Value," Health Catalyst, 2016. https://www.healthcatalyst.com/shift-healthcare-quality-measures-from-volume-to-value. (Accessed on June 13, 2018.)

8. Jared Capo, "Why We Need to Shift Healthcare Quality Measures from Volume to Value," Health Catalyst, 2016. https://www.healthcatalyst.com/shift-healthcare-quality-measures-from-volume-to-value. (Accessed on June 13, 2018.)

9. http://goldcopd.org/about-us/. (Accessed on June 13, 2018.)

10. http://www.heart.org/HEARTORG/. (Accessed on June 13, 2018.)

11. http://www.diabetes.org/. (Accessed on June 13, 2018.)

12. https://www.icsi.org/. (Accessed on June 13, 2018.)

13. Josh Ferguson, "The Who, What, and How of Health Outcome Measures," Presentation by Health Catalyst, 2016. https://www.healthcatalyst.com/the-who-what-and-how-of-health-outcome-measures. (Accessed on June 13, 2018.)

14. Jared Capo, "Why We Need to Shift Healthcare Quality Measures from Volume to Value," Presentation by Health Catalyst, 2016. https://www.healthcatalyst.com/shift-healthcare-quality-measures-from-volume-to-value. (Accessed on June 13, 2018.)

15. Lawrence P. Casalino, et al., "U.S. physician practices spend more than $15.4 billion annually to teport quality measures," *Health Affairs,* March 2016 vol. 35 no. 3 401–406. https://www.healthaffairs.org/doi/abs/10.1377/hlthaff.2015.1258. (Accessed on June 13, 2018.)

16. See, for example, https://www.bcg.com/publications/2015/health-care-payers-providers-how-to-define-health-care-outcomes.aspx. (Accessed on June 13, 2018.)

17. See https://qualitymeasures.ahrq.gov/. (Accessed on June 13, 2018.)

18. The data for Figures 2.1 and 2.2 are taken from the National Quality Measures Clearinghouse of the Agency for Healthcare Research and Quality (AHRQ). Due to funding cutbacks, however, the Clearinghouse data has not been available since July 18, 2018.

19. See, for example, Shannon Williams, "Which Process Improvement Methodology Should You Use?" January 2017. https://www.lucidchart.com/blog/process-improvement-methodologies. (Accessed on June 13, 2018.)

20. See note #14 for source and explanation.

21. "NQR's History," http://www.qualityforum.org/about_nqf/history/. (Accessed on June 13, 2018.)

22. Institute of Medicine. 1997. *The Computer-Based Patient Record: An Essential Technology for Health Care,* Revised Edition. Washington, DC: The National Academies Press. https://doi.org/10.17226/5306. (Accessed on June 13, 2018.)

23. National Institute of Medicine, *To Err is Human: Building a Safer Health System,* 2000.

24. From Molla Sloane Donaldson, Chapter 3, "An Overview of To Err is Human: Re-emphasizing the Message of Patient Safety," appearing in Ronda G Hughes, PhD, MHS, RN. (ed.), *Patient Safety and Quality: An Evidence-Based Handbook for*

Nurses, Rockville (MD): Agency for Healthcare Research and Quality; April 2008, https://www.ncbi.nlm.nih.gov/books/ NBK2673/#ch3.s1. (Accessed on June 13, 2018.)

25. The terms Electronic Medical Record (EMR) and Electronic Health Record (EHR) are often used interchangeably. Technically, an EMR focuses on data collected for diagnosis and treatment in a hospital or physicians' office setting. An EHR encompasses more broadly any data collected about a patient's overall health status, and can contain data collected from sources other than from a patient's physician office or hospital encounter, including data collected by the patient on his/her own. Since these differences are often not reflected or respected by commentators, we will use them as they are found without further exploration into the differences. For an excellent discussion of the technical differences, see Peter Garrett and Joshua Seidman, PhD, "EMR vs EHR – What is the Difference?" *HealthITBuzz* Jan 4, 2011. https://www.healthit. gov/buzz-blog/electronic-health-and-medical-records/emr-vs-ehr-difference/. (Accessed on August 25, 2018.)

26. The ARRA was a stimulus package enacted by the 111th U.S. Congress and signed into law by President Barack Obama in February 2009. Developed in response to the 2008 recession, the ARRA's primary objective was to save existing jobs and create new ones as soon as possible. Other objectives were to provide temporary relief programs for those most affected by the recession and invest in infrastructure, education, health, and renewable energy. The Health Information Technology for Economic and Clinical Health (HITECH) Act was enacted as part of the ARRA, to promote the adoption and meaningful use of health information technology. HITECH allocated $19.2 billion specifically to enhance the acquisition and implementation of Electronic Medical Records.

27. "Meaningful Use and the Shift to the Merit-based Incentive Payment System," https://www.healthit.gov/providers-professionals/how-attain-meaningful-use. (Accessed on June 13, 2018.)

28. Eligible professionals (EP) under the Medicare EHR Incentive Program include: Doctor of medicine or osteopathy, Doctors of dental surgery or dental medicine, Doctors of podiatry, Doctors of optometry, and Chiropractors. The EP definition under the Medicaid EHR Incentive program was broadened to include:

Nurse Practitioners, Certified Nurses/midwives, and Physician Assistants who work in in a Federally Qualified Health Center or Rural Health Clinic that is led by a physician assistant.

29. Excerpted from https://www.cms.gov/Regulations-and-Guidance/Legislation/EHRIncentivePrograms/Stage3Medicaid_Require.html. (Accessed on June 13, 2018.)

30. See, for example, the discussion by Sen. John Thune, Sen. Lamar Alexander, Sen. Pat Roberts, Sen. Richard Burr, Sen. Mike Enzi, "Where Is HITECH's $35 Billion Dollar Investment Going?" *Health Affairs*, March 4, 2015. https://www.healthaffairs.org/do/10.1377/hblog20150304.045199/full/. (Accessed on June 13, 2018.)

Chapter 3

The Unique Role of the Physician

3.1 Introduction

Physicians are likely the most highly educated and compensated "front line" workers of any industry in the American economy. Their interaction with customers (i.e., patients) is essential both to the success of health care organizations generally and to the satisfaction of their customers. In addition, their decisions and recommendations drive much of the revenue that accrues to health care organizations. They expect not only to be accommodated, but to be active participants in the decisions that impact their work—whether that be in developing diagnostic tools, therapeutic regimens, or increasingly in the selection and implementation of information systems that support those activities.

Ironically, a review of a typical hospital or heath system organization chart seldom contains a specifically identified "physician role," except perhaps for a box identifying "medical staff office" or perhaps a physician who coincidently occupies an administrative role. This is yet another fundamental difference that makes health care organizations distinct from organizations in other industries: one of the arguably most important roles in the organization is often not found on the organization chart.

Historically, physicians have owned their own practices and have not worked directly for health care organizations such as hospitals. However, a shift in this employment relationship is underway. For example, the ratio of physician practices owned by hospitals increased from 1 in 7 in 2012, to 1 in 4 just three years later. In addition, 2016 was an inflection year for physician practice ownership in that year it dropped below 50% for the first time.[1] Over the 10-year period between 2000 and 2010, physicians employed by hospitals grew by 34%,[2] and the number of physicians in solo practices declined from over 40% in 1983 to just over 18% in 2012.[3] Who you work for can have a significant impact on what you do, and why, how, and when you do it. These shifts in physician employment status are likely to continue, and in the process contribute to the ongoing complexity of the physician role in health care services.

There are significant differences among physician specialties: how they are practiced, the workflows they use and their data requirements. By some estimates, physicians in the United States currently practice in over 200 specialty and subspecialty areas.[4] Specialties differ by demographic characteristics (e.g., gerontologists vs. pediatricians), whether the practice focuses primarily on diagnostic procedures (e.g., pathologists or radiologists) or therapeutic interventions (e.g., internists or orthopedic surgeons), or whether the focus is on organs (e.g., nephrologists, cardiologists, dermatologists, or ophthalmologists) or diseases (e.g., oncologists or rheumatologists)[5] New specializations are added periodically, such as the recent creation of a new board specialization in Clinical Informatics.[6]

Each of these specialties and subspecialties is defined by a body of knowledge (with much overlap given the focus on human illness and wellness) that is constantly changing as more is learned about the underlying processes of disease diagnosis and therapeutic interventions. While some areas (e.g., subspecialties within a general specialty area) do share common data standards, methods, and requirements for documentation of the care, what is very important to one clinical specialty may be less important to another. What an ophthalmologist requires to document the results of an eye exam, for example, is very different from what an orthopedic surgeon dictates in a joint replacement post-operative note.

The introduction of electronic medical records (EMR) noted in the previous chapter has had to accommodate the inclusion of data from virtually every specialization, making them among the most complex software applications for developers. There is simply no "one size fits all"—and no one "standard" that works for everyone—where EMRs are concerned.

3.2 The Predominance of Knowledge Workers in Health Care

Management guru, Peter Drucker, has offered insight into the physician's role (and by extension, other clinical roles) in health care organizations. He pointed out that the complexity of hospitals was due in large measure to the predominant role played by "Knowledge Workers":

> Above all, Knowledge Workers are not homogenous: Knowledge is effective only if it is specialized. Because knowledge work is specialized, it is deeply splintered work, even in large organizations.[7]

Although Drucker focused on the high degree of specialization among health care workers generally (including billing staff!), given the extent of specialization among physicians, his observations apply equally if not more so to physicians as Knowledge Workers. In fact, he argued that improving the productivity of Knowledge Workers was the most important management goal in any organization.

> The most important contribution management needs
> to make in the twenty-first century is … to increase
> the productivity of KNOWLEDGE WORK and the
> KNOWLEDGE WORKER. [emphasis in original][8]

In part, Drucker was focused on the historical shift in
industries from the manufacturing sector to the services sector, with health care (and its preponderance of Knowledge
Workers) presenting perhaps the greatest challenge.

Drucker was one of the first management theorists to
identify "Knowledge Workers" as a new "class" of workers
that would strongly influence organizational structures and
processes as the 21st century approached. At the time of
his discussion (which originated with his 1969 book, *Age of
Discontinuity*,[9] although references can be found throughout
much of his writing), the focus of performance measurement
was primarily on what could be easily measured at the time:
productivity of workers whose primary task was the creation
of identifiable products and not the provision of services.

Economists' measurement of productivity among the
American work force has historically focused largely on manufacturing processes, since both the input (i.e., factors of production like raw materials and machines to transform materials
in predictable ways) and the output (i.e., specific products like
cars and anything that could be "manufactured") were easily
described, quantified and subsequently aggregated to higher
level, economy-wide metrics. In fact, the transition of the U.S.
economy from one primarily devoted to manufacturing to one
predominated by "services" industries has been a significant
challenge for economists' measurement of productivity. While
most of us can recognize when a "service" has been delivered,
identifying a specific service without the context in which it
has been provided and measuring the quantity and quality of
that service, as noted in Chapter 2, is difficult.

Defining who is and who is not a "Knowledge Worker"
is tricky. Drucker's use of the term appears primarily to

differentiate between workers who use physical factors of production (as noted above, what we typically think of as "raw materials") and workers whose primary production factor is their "knowledge." However, this differentiation has become much less clear over the past several decades as companies have developed ways to improve production processes by asking workers (i.e., tapping into their knowledge) for their views on better ways to do their jobs. In effect, one might now argue that if managed properly, everyone in the organization should be considered a "Knowledge Worker" to some degree.

As work environments become increasingly interdependent, for example, integrating employee contributions with those from robots, it has become evident that employee contributions are essential for an organization to be successful, even to the point of participating in decisions about how the work flow is organized and prioritized. What have historically been "command and control" management structures, with information flowing in one direction, from the top down, are changing to incorporate a much more integrative view of information sources and flows.

> In a collaborative organization … all workers' knowledge counts, regardless of their roles. Every team member contributes, shares knowledge, and participates in making decisions, whether he or she is loading crates, designing products, servicing customer accounts, creating tactical marketing plans, or determining long-term strategy. And most important, information flows in multiple directions rather than cascading from senior leadership down through multiple levels of management to front-line people.[10]

However, before moving too quickly to dismiss the concept of "Knowledge Worker" because it seems that everyone is one to some degree, it is important to note there are specific characteristics of workers whose *primary* production factor is "knowledge."

For example, consider the following definition from Thomas Davenport:

> Knowledge workers have high degrees of expertise, education or experience, and the primary purpose of their jobs involves the creation, distribution, or application of knowledge.[11]

Perhaps the key phrase in this quote is noting "the primary purpose of their jobs," which is simply to acknowledge that while everyone needs to use knowledge in their work, for some members of the work force, knowledge is the "primary" purpose of their job.

Thomas Davenport has also commented on some distinctive characteristics of knowledge workers:

> In such areas life [for the knowledge worker] is less linear; inputs and outputs are less well defined; and information is less "targeted." There are, rather, areas where making sense, interpreting, and understanding are both problematic and highly valued—areas where, above all, meaning and knowledge are at a premium.[12]

Davenport continues this discussion by noting that Knowledge Workers differ from other types of workers in terms of autonomy, motivations, and attitudes. Although he did not specifically use physician examples in describing the characteristics of Knowledge Workers, it is easy to extend his discussion and terminology to physicians.

Knowledge Workers enjoy their autonomy. One must be careful about improvement approaches that impinge on autonomy and the power that comes with it. For example, as electronic clinical pathways become more automated in hospitals with EMRs systems, physicians are

often concerned that their ability to make the best decision on behalf of their patients may be compromised.

Knowledge work tends to be unstructured. Specifying
a detailed flow of work is sometimes possible, but it
is probably not the best way to improve a knowledge
work process. While standardized clinical workflows and
pathways proscribing how physicians should work are
increasingly evident, there is also much resistance from
physicians who feel that their individualized contributions
may be overtaken by methods and processes established
by others.

**Knowledge work often needs to be observed in some
detail** and at some length before it can be truly understood. Physicians often argue that only those with medical training can truly understand what they do and how
they do it; other clinicians such as nurses and pharmacists
often share this view of their own specialties.

Knowledge Workers are usually intelligent and
through training and experience have typically figured
out what works best for them in developing their workflows, so one must be cautious about assuming that
a particular work task is unnecessary, or that a work
process can be improved easily, for example, through
computerization.

Commitment matters to knowledge work. Don't do
anything to damage the Knowledge Worker's commitment
to the job and to the organization, lest one risks losing
the trust of that worker.[13]

The implications of these observations about Knowledge
Workers in health care are straightforward. Using the strictest
definition of the term, it is evident that Knowledge Workers
exist throughout all levels of every health care organization.
With its complexity of processes and structure (as observed
by Drucker), knowledge is a key component and necessary
for every health care worker to be able to perform their jobs

successfully. It is also evident that health care's most expensive and highly educated Knowledge Workers (i.e., physicians) operate within an environment that is highly autonomous, often unstructured in terms of the decisions that need to be made (and the critical timing of those decisions) and have a job that requires extraordinary personal commitment.

Chapter 2 noted that measuring the impact of IT investments in support of improved health care services is a challenge. One aspect of that challenge is the fact that these services are delivered by Knowledge Workers, whose characteristics would seem to run counter to the areas in which IT investments have historically been most successful, i.e., the introduction of computers into highly routinized work processes and establishing automated processes in which worker autonomy is limited.[14] On the other hand, as the workers with the greatest impact on the care being provided daily, physicians in particular represent the most important constituency for delivering value from information technology investments in health care.

3.3 Changes in the Physician Role

The traditional model of the physician's role is straightforward: the patient directly seeks the care of a physician, whether in his/her office or in a hospital setting. The physician determines the appropriate diagnosis and with the assistance and support of a broad ranging group of assistants (e.g., nurses, pharmacists, social workers, etc.) oversees the treatment of the patient. Throughout this process, the physician is "in charge;" S/he is the driver of all activity surrounding the care of the patient, e.g., determining what procedures should be performed on the patient, reviewing the results of radiological or laboratory work, writing orders for medications, etc. But this historically defined role as the master of all care provided to the patient is changing, and with it more complexity is being introduced into the health care services process.

The American Association of Medical Colleges (AAMC) has projected that under most future scenarios, a physician shortage is likely in the future, regardless of the growth in the numbers of advanced practice nurses, physician assistants, or the likely expansion of alternative sites of care such as retail clinics, urgent care centers, or even the rise of more integrated delivery models such as Accountable Care Organizations.[15] Recent workforce projections indicate that the demand for physicians will exceed the supply, with shortages of between 40,800 and 104,900 physicians by 2030—the lower estimate reflecting possible changes in health care delivery patterns, the growth of non-physician clinicians and possible delayed retirement for current physicians.

Projected physician shortages, however, may be tempered to some extent by the growth in the numbers of Nurse Practitioners (NP), perhaps the most likely potential disrupter to the traditional physician role. There are close to a quarter million NPs currently licensed in the United States, representing a near doubling of NPs over the past 10 years.[16] Nurse Practitioners hold prescriptive licenses in all 50 states, and can administer controlled substances in 49 states. However, states differ in defining the actual tasks that NPs can perform:

> In full practice states, NPs are able to assess patients, diagnose conditions, order diagnostic exams, and provide treatments under the authority of their regional state board of nursing. Reduced practice states require collaboration with another health-care provider in at least one aspect of NP practice. Restricted practice states—concentrated mainly in the Pacific Northwest—require direct supervision or team management of at least one element of NP practice.[17]

The growth of the NP role is not without controversy. At the June 2017 meeting of the House of Delegates of the American Medical Association (AMA), a resolution to place

"APRNs (Advanced Practice Registered Nurses) under state medical board and regulatory control with AMA developing model state legislation" failed by a margin to 254–204—close to a 50/50 split.[18]

In addition to the disruption brought by the rise of Nurse Practitioners, traditional facilities in which care has been provided are also being challenged. Physicians' offices and hospitals have been traditional sites of health care services, but more recently the rise of retail clinics (which typically do not have a physician on site), urgent care centers, and hospital-owned ambulatory care centers, have challenged the dominance of single or multi-specialty group practice facilities. The urgent care market has grown approximately 20% over the past four years, and currently has close to 10,000 clinics producing $15 billion in revenue.[19]

The retail drugstore chain CVS, for example, now operates 1,100 Minute Clinics in 33 states and represents about half of all retail clinics in the United States, with the goal of having a clinic within 10 minutes of half of the U.S. population.[20] Walgreens has over 370 clinics,[21] and Kroger's Little Clinic has over 215 locations.[22]

The provision of health care services is no longer the single province of the physician; care is being provided in settings outside of the traditional physician office and hospital suite, in some cases by clinicians who have never been to medical school. How does the patient decide where to seek care and from whom to seek it? It is no longer simply, "call the doctor," as more options are available and more locations and facilities for care are being developed and offered on terms often more convenient to the patient. With the disruption and dispersion of traditional roles and locations, the "Knowledge Worker" designation can now be applied to roles beyond physicians practicing in their offices, and the challenge of improving services through the introduction of IT has become even more challenging. One major implication of these changes is that health care complexity continues to increase not diminish.[23]

3.4 IT Support of Knowledge Workers

The characteristics of Knowledge Workers make them especially challenging to support with information technology. As was noted earlier, physicians and other clinicians are likely the quintessential examples of Knowledge Workers; computers are not yet well suited to support and improve the services that Knowledge Workers provide.

The value criteria for information technology investments supporting Knowledge Workers in general must reflect the special characteristics that these workers bring to organizational processes: autonomy, lack of structure, and expectations about having access to the growing variety, complexity, and sheer volume of data that enables intelligent Knowledge Workers to be successful in what they do. Value can be found only to the extent that routine processes can be automated without impinging on the Knowledge Workers' sense of autonomy, intelligence and commitment. EMRs, perhaps the most extensive (and expensive) IT investment supporting physicians, have often led to dissatisfaction and frustration, especially with the standardization of processes which they often and most easily support.[24]

A 2016 study conducted by the Mayo Clinic surveyed over 6,000 clinicians in active practice, almost 85% of whom used electronic health records (EHRs) in their practice and a similar percentage used the specific functionality of Computerized Physician Order Entry (CPOE). The primary conclusion is striking: "Physicians who used EHRs and CPOE had lower satisfaction with the amount of time spent on clerical tasks and higher rates of burnout … ."[25]

Another recent survey of over 500 responding primary care physicians provided additional levels of detail[26]:

- 74% felt that using an EHR added additional hours to their workday.
- 71% agreed that EHRs greatly contribute to physician burnout.

- 69% felt that using an EHR takes time away from patients.
- 63% believed EHRs have led to improved care.
- 49% thought that using an EHR detracted from their clinical effectiveness.
- 44% thought that the primary value of EHRs is for data storage.
- 40% believed that there are more challenges with EHRs than benefits.

One additional finding was that only 8% of the respondents said that the primary value of their EHR was "clinically related," a statistic that raises significant questions about whether EHRs are accomplishing what they are designed to do, which is to improve patient care.

Nurses (who also approximate the "Knowledge Worker" definition) are another clinical group impacted by information technology investments. In a 40-state survey of nearly 14,000 licensed registered nurses who have used EHRs for at least six months, negative experiences appear even more prominent than with the physicians': 92% of nurses surveyed expressed dissatisfaction with their inpatient EHR systems; 85% of nurses struggle with continually flawed EHR systems; and 88% blame financial administrators and CIOs for selecting low performance systems based on EHR pricing, government incentives, and cutting corners at the expense of quality of care.[27]

Computers work best when supporting work processes that are highly structured; they have historically been most effective when tasks are standardized and consistent with predictable inputs leading to predictable outputs. Knowledge Workers, particularly those involved in clinical processes in health care, represent the opposite. While "standards of care" provide guidelines developed by professional societies for caring for particular types of patients, there is of necessity much about caring for patients that requires deviation from those guidelines, because patients often deviate from the categories described by the "standards of care" guidelines. Patients are hardly "predictable inputs," although all the while hoping for "predictable outputs" such as the curing of their disease. This is not the optimal environment for computerization.

The other challenge with physicians as Knowledge Workers is that they are extraordinarily resistant to change. The intensive hours of training both in medical school and through residency create a mindset of responsibility and a reliance on "what was learned in medical school." Physicians typically practice how they were trained, and their training impacts how they practice throughout their careers—an indication of the intensity of that training. Changing ingrained practice patterns presents a substantial challenge. A common question asked when two physicians meet for the first time is, "Where did you train?"—signaling the importance of medical training and its lasting impact on how a physician practices.

Decisions about how a patient should be cared for are often made by a physician acting on his or her own judgment, many times under significant time constraints, which tends to favor both the physician's own experience as to "what has worked before," and the rigorous training they received. The culture of health care, as a result, tends to be conservative, resistant to change, whether that involves new drugs or treatments or new administrative policies. Medical "breakthroughs" are the exception and may be readily embraced, although the time frame of translating new discoveries into actual clinical practice can take years. The process of moving from science to clinical practice can be lengthy, and physicians as scientists want data to demonstrate the efficiency of any new treatments, processes, programs, or policies before putting them into practice.

Much has been made of the potential contributions of newly developed data collection, management and analytic software such as IBM's Watson initiative, which purports to provide continued improvement in the ability to diagnose and recommend treatment regimens for certain types of illnesses. However, the long run impact of this type of initiative is still unclear given how these systems "learn" (most often from historical experiences), the skills required to use this technology effectively and the associated costs of providing it.[28] In addition, it is important to note that health care is a ways away from replacing the role of the physician and other care givers in diagnostic and treatment processes:

> Conversations these days about the "future of medicine" tend to stray toward novel pharmaceuticals, toward big data analytics and A.I. healthbots, toward genomics and microbiomics and all other manner of -omicses. Neglected in all of this chatter is the enduring power of the human caregiver—the fact that the effectiveness of medicine, even today, remains bound up with how perceptively it is administered, and by whom. ... [S]o many forms of healing still require a human hand.[29]

While it is true that EMRs have facilitated the collection and storage of vast amounts of data related to the care of patients, providing that data to physicians in a format and structure that can be used at the point of the service transaction—which one might argue is where the real value needs to occur and the Knowledge Worker can be most effective—appears not to be happening, at least according to those physicians who have expressed their dissatisfaction with EMRs.

All of this continues to expand on the essential point of this and the previous chapter: the combination of services and the delivery of those services by Knowledge Workers continues to be an area in which IT investments have yet to demonstrate value as measured through improved outcomes, either to the Knowledge Workers themselves or to the patients to whom they provide service. Two of the foundational factors contributing to the complexity of the health care industry have therefore been established: (1) the predominance of services versus the creation of products;

and (2) the use of Knowledge Workers whose expectations of autonomy and lack of structured work processes create an environment that is not only highly complex but very challenging for the successful introduction of computerized capabilities.

Notes

1. Brenden Murphy, "For First Time, Physician Practice Owners Are Not the Majority," AMA Wire, May 31, 2017 https://wire.ama-assn.org/practice-management/first-time-physician-practice-owners-are-not-majority. (Accessed June 14, 2018.)
2. Richard Gunderman, "Should Doctors Work for Hospitals?" *The Atlantic*, May 27, 2014. https://www.theatlantic.com/health/archive/2014/05/should-doctors-work-for-hospitals/371638/. (Accessed June 14, 2018.)
3. Robert Lowes, "1 in 2 Physicians Still Self-Employed as Hospitals Beckon," *Medscape Medical News*, September 18, 2013. https://www.medscape.com/viewarticle/811213. (Accessed June 14, 2018.)
4. American Association of Medical Colleges, Center for Workforce Studies, 2008 Physician Specialty Data, November 2008. https://www.aamc.org/download/47352/data. (Accessed June 14, 2018.)
5. For more information on medical specialties, see https://www.aamc.org/cim/specialty/exploreoptions/list/. (Accessed June 14, 2018.)
6. The formal Clinical Informatics Board Certification process was initiated by the American Medical Informatics Association in 2007 and approved by the American Board of Medical Specialty in 2011. Currently more than 1,400 physicians have received this certification.
7. See the classic article by Peter Drucker, "They're Not Employees, They're People," *Harvard Business Review*, February 2002, p. 74. https://hbr.org/2002/02/theyre-not-employees-theyre-people. (Accessed June 14, 2018.)
8. See, for example, Peter Drucker, *Management Challenges for the 21st Century*. Oxford: Butterworth-Heinemann, 1999, p. 135. (Emphasis in original.)

9. Peter F. Drucker, *Age of Discontinuity: Guidelines to Our Changing Society.* New York: Harper, 1969.

10. Evan Rosen, "Every Worker Is a Knowledge Worker," *Bloomberg BusinessWeek*, January 11, 2011. https://www.bloomberg.com/news/articles/2011-01-11/every-worker-is-a-knowledge-worker. (Accessed June 14, 2018.)

11. Thomas H. Davenport, *Thinking for a Living, How to Get Better Performance and Results from Knowledge Workers.* Boston: Harvard University Press, 2005, p. 10.

12. Thomas H. Davenport, *Thinking for a Living, How to Get Better Performance and Results from Knowledge Workers.* Boston: Harvard University Press, 2005, p. 15.

13. Thomas H. Davenport, *Thinking for a Living, How to Get Better Performance and Results from Knowledge Workers.* Boston: Harvard University Press, 2005, p. 24. Headings are from Davenport; discussions are the author's.

14. Alvaro Rocha, et al., "Approaches and State of the Art," in *New Advances in Information Systems and Technologies*, Vol 1, Springer International, 2016, p. 457ff.

15. American Association of Medical Colleges, "Physician Supply and Demand through 2030: Key Findings," based on "2017 Update: The Complexities of Physician Supply and Demand: Projections from 2015 to 2030," see https://news.aamc.org/press-releases/article/workforce_projections_03142017/. (Accessed June 14, 2018.)

16. American Association of Nurse Practitioners. https://www.aanp.org/about-aanp. (Accessed June 14, 2018.)

17. American Association of Nurse Practitioners. https://www.nurse-practitionerschools.com/faq/what-is-np. (Accessed June 14, 2018.)

18. Nicole Livanos, JD, MPP, "Physicians Look to Disrupt Longtime Regulatory Tradition for APRNs," *Journal of Nursing Regulation, October 2017* Volume 8, Issue 3, pp. 59–62. http://www.journalofnursingregulation.com/article/S2155-8256(17)30161-8/fulltext. (Accessed June 14, 2018.)

19. Kalorama Information Reports, "Riding Wave of Consumerism, Urgent Care Market Hits $15 Billion," *Healthcare Finance News*, April 5, 2017. http://www.healthcarefinancenews.com/news/riding-wave-consumerism-urgent-care-market-hits-15-billion-kalorama-information-reports. (Accessed June 14, 2018.)

20. "What's Next for MinuteClinic," https://cvshealth.com/thought-leadership/whats-next-for-minuteclinic. (Accessed June 14, 2018.)

21. https://www.walgreens.com/pharmacy/healthcare-clinic/locations.jsp. (Accessed June 14, 2018.)

22. https://www.prnewswire.com/news-releases/krogers-the-little-clinic-provides-added-convenience-with-well-hold-your-spot-300408810.html. (Accessed June 14, 2018.)

23. See, for example, "Merger Medicine and the Disappearing Doctor," *The New York Times*, April 8, 2018. https://www.nytimes.com/2018/04/22/opinion/retail-clinics.html. (Accessed June 14, 2018.)

24. See, for example, "Is Physician Dissatisfaction with EHR Use on the Rise?" https://ehrintelligence.com/news/is-physician-dissatisfaction-with-ehr-use-on-the-rise (accessed on June 26, 2018), and "Electronic Health Record Use a Bitter Pill for Many Physicians," *Perspectives in Health Information Management*, Winter 2016. Published online January 1, 2016. https://www.ncbi.nlm.nih.gov/pmc/articles/PMC4739443/. (accessed June 14, 2018.)

25. Tait D. Shanafelt, MD, et al., "Relationship between Clerical Burden and Characteristics of the Electronic Environment with Physician Burnout and Professional Satisfaction," *Mayo Clinic Proceedings, July 2016*, Volume 91, Issue 7, pp. 836–848. http://www.mayoclinicproceedings.org/article/S0025-6196(16)30215-4/abstract. (Accessed June 14, 2018.)

26. "How Doctors Feel about Electronic Health Records," A National Physician Poll by Stanford Medicine and The Harris Poll, March 2018. http://med.stanford.edu/content/dam/sm/ehr/documents/EHR-Poll-Presentation.pdf. (Accessed June 12, 2018.)

27. For further information on this survey, see "Hospital Nurses Forced to Develop Creative Workarounds to Deal with EHR System Flaws: Outdated Technologies and Lack of Interoperability," *BlackBook Market Research*, October 16, 2014, https://blackbookmarketresearch.newswire.com/press-release/hospital-nurses-forced-to-develop-creative-workarounds-to-deal. (Accessed June 14, 2018.)

28. See, for example, Drake Bennett, "BM's Artificial Intelligence Problem, or Why Watson Can't Get a Job," *Bloomberg*, January 10, 2014, http://www.bloomberg.com/bw/articles/2014-01-10/ibms-artificial-intelligence-problem-or-why-watson-cant-get-a-job (Accessed June 14, 2018), and "IBM Pitched Its Watson Supercomputer as a Revolution in Cancer Care. It's Nowhere Close," September 5, 2017, https://www.

statnews.com/2017/09/05/watson-ibm-cancer/. (Accessed June 14, 2018.) See also David H. Freedman, "A Reality Check for IBM's AI Ambitions," *MIT Technology Review*, June 27, 2017. https://www.technologyreview.com/s/607965/a-reality-check-for-ibms-ai-ambitions/. (Accessed on June 23, 2018.)

29. The Health Issue, Introduction, *The New York Times*, May 20, 2018, p. 31. https://www.nytimes.com/issue/magazine/2018/05/25/052018-issue. (Accessed on September 20, 2018.)

Chapter 4

Patients as Challenging Customers

4.1 Introduction

In the health care industry, patients are considered the ultimate customers—the persons who in the end are the recipients of the services that the health care industry delivers, and in many ways, are the reason the industry exists at all.

As with just about any "service" encounter, the quality of the service can be improved to the extent that the receiver of the service (i.e., the customer) *actively* participates in the transaction. This might include providing information about the history or current status of a customer's situation, preferences about what service is needed as well as a commitment to follow-up and take actions that may be deemed necessary based on the service. This is no less true in health care, where it is assumed that the extent to which the patient actively participates in a health care service can have an impact on the outcome. Beyond participating in the actual encounter between the physician and the patient, as a customer the patient may also be expected to provide information regarding symptoms, and subsequently to follow post-encounter instructions or take prescribed medications.

A report from the Robert Wood Johnson Foundation succinctly states both the hope and the challenges for consumers (i.e., patients as customers) actively participating in their own health care. The report notes that:

> informed and engaged consumers have a vital role to play in improving the quality of care that the U.S. health system delivers to patients. ... [W]hen consumers are armed with the right information, they will demand high-quality services from their providers, choose treatment options wisely, and become active participants and self-managers of their own health and health care. Yet the choices ... are becoming *increasingly complex* along with the health care system itself. [emphasis added][1]

Involving patients in their own care—also known as "patient engagement"—has become a mantra in the health care policy community. In fact, two of the core measures for meeting the goals of the federal government's Meaningful Use initiative[2] have relied on getting patients more involved in their own care by providing patients with access to their own medical data:

Objective:
Provide patients the ability to view online, download, and transmit their health information within four business days of the information being available to the EP [Eligible Provider].

Measure:
Measure 1 – More than 50% of all unique patients seen by the EP during the EHR (electronic health record) reporting period are provided timely (available to the patient within four business days after the information

is available to the EP) online access to their health information.

Measure 2 – More than 5% of all unique patients seen by the EP during the EHR reporting period (or their authorized representatives) view, download, or transmit to a third party their health information.[3]

Health care organizations and information technology (IT) companies have responded to this initiative with products designed to provide patients with access to their own data, largely through patient "portals."[4]

4.2 Providing Patient Access to Their Medical Data

In many ways, patient portals represent a sensible way to give patients access to their own health data. Rather than having to pour through reams of paper that have historically constituted a patient's medical record, why not just make that data available on line, through a dedicated website that patients can access with a unique identifier and password? Unfortunately, while the process seems straightforward, and the technology readily available, the success of the patient portal strategy has fallen short of expectations.

Table 4.1 illustrates the types of patient information available through hospital and clinical professional (generally physician office) patient portals. These metrics indicate that for the most part, data that is required to meet Meaningful Use standards is in fact available. Where that data is not specifically mandated (e.g., clinician notes, immunization history, radiology images, and result reports) the availability is much less.

On the other hand, just because the data is available through a portal does not mean that patients are accessing their data. Figure 4.1 illustrates this point: the percentage of patients who appear to use patient portals is quite small.

Table 4.1   Estimated Percentages of Providers that Routinely Offer Various Types of Health Information through Patient Portals

Type of Health Information	Required for Meaningful Use?	% Hospitals Offering	% Health Care Professionals Offering
Allergies	Yes	92%	81%
Clinical history	Yes	83%	77%
Clinician notes	No	46%	54%
Current medications	Yes	92%	82%
Immunization history	No	82%	67%
Laboratory test results	Yes	94%	77%
Problems/conditions	Yes	91%	80%
Radiology images	No	13%	31%
Radiology result reports	No	79%	65%
After-visit summary	Yes	85%	77%

Source: Health Information Technology: HHS Should Assess the Effectiveness of Its Efforts to Enhance Patient Access to and Use of Electronic Health Information, GAO-17-305, March 2017, p. 13. https://www.gao.gov/products/GAO-17-305. (Accessed June 14, 2018.)

When patients are questioned directly about why they do not make more use of portals, several responses are typical:

1. Not all their data is available through the portal.
2. Data from hospital stays and physician visits often require accessing separate portals.
3. Historical data that was collected and stored in paper medical records is not available through the portal.

A recent poll focusing on older Americans found that about half had actually set up a patient portal for themselves. Women more often set up a portal than men, and those with some college education and those with higher incomes are more likely to

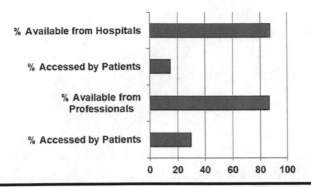

Figure 4.1 Availability and access of patient records. (From: Health Information Technology: HHS Should Assess the Effectiveness of Its Efforts to Enhance Patient Access to and Use of Electronic Health Information, GAO-17-305, March 2017, pp. 14–17. https://www.gao. gov/assets/690/683388.pdf. Accessed June 14, 2018.)

set up a portal than those with high school education and lower incomes.[5] Although these percentages are somewhat higher than reported in Figure 4.1, in general close to half of all patients do not setup or access their patient data through patient portals.

4.3 Telemedicine

Another information technology investment that appears to have promise for reaching out to patients is telemedicine—the capability of connecting patients in their homes to care givers in their offices through both voice and data telecommunications. While initially focused on establishing video links between patients and their care givers, telemedicine has grown to include not just virtual visits but also remote monitoring using a variety of data collection and educational tools. Height, weight, blood pressure, video images, patient education, electrocardiogram (ECG) data, and blood glucose monitoring are just a few of the devices and capabilities currently in use.

Telemedicine can provide significant benefits to patients, including better access for patients (especially those unable to leave their homes), reduction in costs (with remote patient monitoring and subsequent transfer of data directly to the care giver), greater compliance of patients with prescribed treatment regimens (due to remote monitoring) and greater access to care should emergencies arise.[6]

Traditional telecommunications companies such as Verizon and AT&T have made major commitments to the telemedicine market. Large technology companies such as Google are also making investments. Some projections indicate that the overall telemedicine market is likely to grow from $230 million in 2013 to an estimated $1.9 billion by 2018. In 2016, 1.2 million virtual visits were recorded, and it is estimated that over 70% of hospitals and more than 50% of physicians' groups have established some form of telemedicine program. The percentage of large employers offering some type of telemedicine benefits has grown from 48% in 2015 to an estimated 74% in 2016. As an example, through ClickWell Care, Stanford Medicine's telemedicine program, patients can choose to meet with their health care providers over the phone, via video conferencing or in person. At the end of the program's first year, an estimated 55%–60% of all clinic visits were managed virtually.[7]

4.4 Patients Are Challenged to Understand Their Medical Conditions

Many companies entering the health care industry have focused initially on the patient as consumer and have developed products intended to be sold directly to them.[8] However, a recent survey of entrepreneurs in the digital health market noted that 34% started with a business to consumer (B2C) business model, but 61% eventually changed to either B2B2C (a hybrid model of B2B and B2C) or simply a business to business (B2B) model. Only 14% attempted to retain a B2C model and the largest investments continue to focus on B2B.[9]

At least two major issues challenge Business to Consumer (B2C) revenue models and expectations for significant consumer engagement in health care: (1) consumers in health care seldom pay for many of the services they receive; and (2) consumers as patients often have neither the interest nor the capacity to be actively engaged in their own health care.

Getting paid for health care services in America today is an extraordinarily complex and often time-consuming process, and consumers typically neither pay for the full costs of their care nor understand much about the payment process. A 2013 study by the American Medical Association found that on average, patients pay less than 25% of the amount that insurers billed physicians for providing health care services.[10]

Several studies have documented patients' general lack of understanding about their health care insurance policies, and the data are striking: only 23% understood policy terminology, 36% understood what a Health Maintenance Organization (HMO) is, 20% knew what a Preferred Provider Organization (PPO) is and only 11% were familiar with Health Savings Accounts (HSAs).[11] Terms such as co-insurance, deductibles and benefit maximums were similarly baffling.[12] These findings point to the challenges faced by everyone involved in the health care marketplace, especially if they are assuming consumers will bear the cost of products in an industry in which they have had little experience (and often little expectation) of doing so.

In addition to the challenges about consumers paying for health care products, there are concerns about whether these individuals have the interest or even the capacity to participate in ways that bring value to the health care encounter.

In looking at how active consumers are involved in their own health care, a Research Brief from the Center for Studying Health System Change (HSC) made a strong statement with broad assumptions and implications:

> There is a growing consensus that activating and engaging consumers is an essential component to health care reform in the United States. The health care choices of individual consumers and daily management

of their own health can profoundly affect health care utilization, costs and outcomes.… [M]ost health care reformers at least acknowledge that improvements in quality, cost containment and reductions in low-value care will not occur without more informed and engaged consumers and patients.[13]

The HSC moved beyond assumptions about why consumer involvement was important to attempting to measure just how active consumers were in participating in their own health care. The study identified four levels of patient activation[14]:

Level 1 – Least activated level, with participation labeled as "passive" and lacking confidence to play an active role in their care.

Level 2 – Lacking basic knowledge and confidence in one's ability to participate.

Level 3 – Able to take some action, but lacking confidence and skill to participate in all necessary behaviors.

Level 4 – Most activated level, able to support the health care process even though perhaps not able to maintain such support in the face of "life stressors."

Even with so many assumptions being made about how important it is for consumers to actively participate in their own health care, the data in Figure 4.2 indicate that less than half of U.S. adults participate at what HSC has defined as Level 4 Activation, the highest level.

It is also evident from Figure 4.2 that activation levels never rise above 45%, for any specified age range, even for persons at the highest level of activation (Level 4). What is disconcerting about this data is that while older persons tend to be sicker than younger persons, they participate less in their care—understandable, perhaps, but of concern if you agree with the assertion that participating in one's health care is important in terms of "quality, cost containment and reductions in low value care."[15]

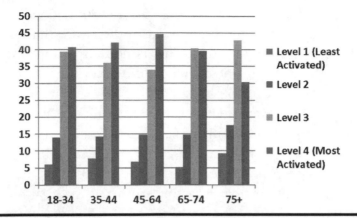

Figure 4.2   Level of activation U.S. adults by age. (Data from "How Engaged Are Consumers in Their Health and Health Care and Why Does It Matter?" Center for Studying Health System Change, No. 8, October 2008. http://www.hschange.org/CONTENT/1019/. [Accessed June 14, 2018.] Used with permission.)

In addition to age-related participation levels, it is helpful to look at levels of Activation for persons with chronic conditions, since one might reasonably assume that persons who suffer from chronic illnesses would exhibit higher levels of participation in their health care. Data from the HSC study for this breakdown are indicated in Figure 4.3.

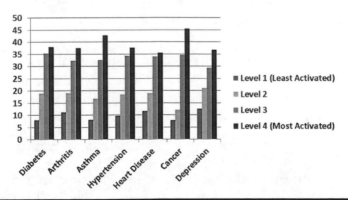

Figure 4.3   Level of activation U.S. adults with chronic conditions. (Data from "How Engaged Are Consumers in Their Health and Health Care and Why Does It Matter?" Center for Studying Health System Change, No. 8, October 2008. http://www.hschange.org/ CONTENT/1019/. [Accessed June 14, 2018.] Used with permission.)

Figure 4.3 indicates that patients with chronic conditions tend to be somewhat more involved in their care than age grouping alone would predict. This is not surprising since if you have a persistent illness that requires periodic monitoring (daily in some cases), you must participate in your own care. But it is perhaps surprising that even for cancer patients, who top the chronically ill group of Level 4 Activation, only 45% function at Level 4.

The message from these findings seems clear: as much as we think that patients participating in their own health care is essential to achieving better outcomes and lower costs, the fact is that participation is not occurring at very high levels, even for patients whose health conditions (e.g., chronic illnesses) would seem to have the greatest benefit from their participation.

The HSC study is a useful source for understanding how patients' participation in their own health care varies by age and chronicity of illness, but it does not provide insight into the actual capability of patients to participate in their care. The Agency for Healthcare Research and Quality (AHRQ) released a study in 2008 based on data collected several years earlier and reported in their 2007 *National Healthcare Disparities Report*. In this study, the AHRQ noted that in the general population,

14% had *below basic* skills: accomplish only simple tasks such as understanding a set of short instructions or identifying what is permissible to drink before a medical test.

22% had *basic* skills: read a pamphlet to understand two reasons why a disease test might be appropriate despite a lack of symptoms.

53% had *intermediate* skills: read instructions on a prescription label to determine the right time to take medication.

12% of adults had *proficient* skills: weigh the risks and benefits of different treatments, know how to calculate health insurance costs, and able to fill out complex medical forms.[16] [emphasis added]

In summary, at the time of this study, fully 36% of the population had only basic or below basic skills—the low end of the scale, while at the higher end, only 12% had proficient skills, which are essential to actively participate in the management of one's own health care. While access to the internet may have increased the level of "health care literacy" among the U.S. adult population somewhat since this study was published, given the variability in accuracy and quality of internet-based health care information, one might assume that there probably have not been significant changes.

In fact, where patients get their health care information has not changed significantly over the past several years, even with many more sources and, through the internet, more access. Another recent study noted little change in patients using the internet and contacting friends and relatives between 2007 and 2010, but the use of hardcopy books, magazines and newspapers dropped by nearly half, from 36% to 18%. In general, older patients, those with chronic illnesses and those with lower educational levels tend to seek information on a less frequent basis.[17]

More recent studies confirm the data about the challenges patients face in actively participating in their own care:

- 18% of adults are considered "health literate" versus 17% who are "profoundly health illiterate" and 65% "somewhat illiterate." (Data from a 2016 iTriage survey of 1,000 adults commissioned by Aetna).[18]
- 56% of adults (the Content and Compliant, Casual and Cautious segments) are not inclined to educate themselves, a number that decreased only slightly from 59% since 2008 (Deloitte Center for Health Solutions 2015 Survey of Health Consumers).[19]

As if to add to the challenges of involving patients in their own care, even the popular press cites statistics about patients' lack of follow-through and their inability to comply with their physicians' recommendations. For example, it is not uncommon for 20%–30% of patients to neglect to fill medication prescriptions, and typically half of medications for chronic diseases are not taken as per the physician's prescription. Unfilled prescriptions are estimated to cost America's health care industry between $100 billion and $289 billion annually.[20]

By any account, the facts about patients' participation in their own care are discouraging. While there may be a myriad of reasons (often highly individualized) for why there is such a lack of participation, even among persons with chronic conditions, and even with the assumption that higher levels of participation lead to better, more effective and efficient outcomes, the fact remains that this situation adds to the complexity of providing care. And while patient portals, telemedicine, and home-based medical devices all seek to minimize this complexity by providing opportunities for participation and seeking to make participation easier and more convenient, it remains a significant challenge.

4.5 Are "Wearables" a Solution to Patient Compliance?

Another growing area of patient participation is "wearables." Wearables generally enable patients to collect data on their personal activities and send that data to clinicians or simply store the data for their own review. In these situations, the data collection is a by-product of a particular activity so other than wearing the device, there is little effort needed by the patient to collect the data.

Health devices constitute the primary use of most wearables on the market today. Market analysts describe four segments in this area:

- **Lifestyle and fitness** include fitness trackers, activity trackers, and sports trackers. Personal health monitoring has been a large contributor to this arena and continues to blend the lines between medical devices and lifestyle devices. Although many of the lifestyle and fitness devices are not technically medical devices, the U.S. Food and Drug Administration (FDA) has defined them as general wellness devices.

■ **Diagnostics and monitoring** include devices that perform glucose monitoring; cardiovascular monitoring and event recording; pregnancy, obstetrics, fetal, and infant monitoring; neurological monitoring, such as electroencephalogram (EEG) tests; and sleep monitoring devices.

■ **Therapeutic devices** monitor disease states and track health activity, store data, and deliver feedback therapy for activities such as respiratory therapy, insulin management, and pain management.

■ **Injury prevention and rehabilitation devices** are typically non-invasive and focus on injury prevention and rehabilitation by measuring body motion, wearing a sensing garment, and registering fall detection.

The amount of data collected by wearables is significant. To cite just one example, a continuous glucose monitoring (CGM) wearable for diabetics can generate almost 300 data points each day or close to 110,000 data points annually—and that is measuring just one set of data for one patient on a daily basis. Close to 30 million people have been diagnosed with diabetes in the United States, and if only half of those use a CGM, this group alone would generate 1.65E12 data points annually.[21]

Some estimates indicate that by 2018 more than 130 million wearable devices will be shipped on a worldwide basis, and more than 578 million wearables will be in use by 2019 and most of these will be used to measure some aspect of health. But even with the volume of data collected by devices on behalf of patients, it remains a challenge to understand what this data means and how to use it to improve a person's health. As one observer noted some years ago,

> Our ability to use computer technology to capture,
> store, retrieve, and reproduce data, wildly surpasses
> our ability to use technology to help analyse [sic],
> refine, and render more manageable the mass of data
> which data processing has spawned. We are great at
> getting information in, but not so good at extracting
> the information that we want.[22]

This problem has been labeled as the "Technology Lag,"
the gap between collecting and "processing" data and the ability to gain knowledge from that data. The explosion in health
care data (documented in more detail in Chapter 6) may indicate that our ability to "extract the information we want" may
be getting harder not easier.

4.6 Patients' Use of Information Technology

The key transactional relationship in health care is the one
that occurs between the physician and the patient. Despite
the technological advances that have occurred both inside
and outside of health care, the true test of success in this
industry is what impact investments such as information technology have on the lives of patients. It is easy to
become fascinated by technology, and the extraordinary
developments that have occurred over the past several
years—unfortunately in many cases forgetting that in health
care, it is the effect on patients that is the ultimate test of
success. All involved in health care need to keep the IT
focus where it belongs, on the patient, regardless of the dis-
tractions of technology.

The health care experience can be daunting for any patient,
whether the purpose is an annual physical exam or the need
for a diagnosis and treatment of an ache or a pain that seems
out of the ordinary. It is not only that we often do not understand what ails us, but that the encounter between a patient

and a clinician is arguably one of the most personal and intimate that one can have.

Information technology in health care is expected to enhance both the quality (i.e., the effectiveness) of the transaction between the clinician and the patient and at the same time make that encounter more efficient. There is general agreement that the more a patient is involved in their own care, the better the outcome and presumably the more efficient as well. That said, engaging a patient in his or her own health care service can be a challenge, whether due to a patient's lack of understanding about what ails them, a patient's inability to engage due to age or infirmity, or at the extreme, a complete lack of consciousness. And information technology investments to date have not seemed to lessen these challenges.

Information technology solutions abound when it comes to proposing ways to engage patients in their own care. The creation of patient portals, for example, seems like an excellent way to provide patients with greater access to their health care data—if only they would use them. But even if usage increases, there is no guarantee that patients would understand the content of the data that they are able to access.

4.7 Patient Concerns about Their Data

Patients are increasingly concerned about how their data is being managed: more than half of all consumers have concerns about the range of health care information technologies, including patient portals, mobile apps and electronic health records, and by 2017, 70% appeared to distrust health technology generally, up sharply from just 10% in 2014. Over 90% of patients are also worried about how their personal health data is being managed, including prescriptions and mental health notes. As a result, close to 90% acknowledge withholding information from their personal physicians, and close to

70% are concerned about whether their primary care physician actually understands the technology s/he is using.[23]

All of this goes back to the challenge of the uniqueness of patients as customers in the health care industry, and the complexity that patients add to the industry. They are reluctant participants in their own health care, even though participation is essential to quality service. They are increasingly concerned about what is happening to the data that records their health care experiences, yet they are being asked to provide increasing amounts of data in support of both the diagnostic and treatment processes in which they participate.

New developments in information technology such as wearables generate vast amounts of data on a patient's health status, but we still fall short in our ability to analyze the data that is being generated. This underscores one of the underlying themes emphasized throughout this book: while IT investments continue to accelerate across industries, there are many unique aspects to IT investments in health care that truly separate it from every other industry in our economy.

Notes

1. Sharon B. Arnold, "Improving Quality Health Care: The Role of Consumer Engagement," Robert Wood Johnson Foundation, October 2007, p. 1. https://www.rwjf.org/en/library/research/2007/10/improving-quality-health-care.html. (Accessed June 14, 2018.)
2. See Chapter 2 for more details on the federal government's Meaningful Use initiative.
3. https://www.cms.gov/Regulations-and-Guidance/Legislation/EHRIncentivePrograms/downloads/Stage2_EPCore_7_PatientElectronicAccess.pdf. (Accessed June 14, 2018.)
4. A patient portal is a secure online website that gives patients convenient 24-hour access to personal health information from anywhere with an internet connection. Using a secure

username and password, patients can view health information such as recent doctor visits, discharge summaries, medications, lab results, as well as to exchange secure e-mail with their health care teams, request prescription refills, check benefits and coverage, make payments, etc., and view educational materials.

5. University of Michigan National Poll on Healthy Aging, March 2018. https://www.healthyagingpoll.org/sites/default/files/2018-05/NPHA_Patient-Portal_051418__1.pdf. (Accessed on June 12, 2018.)

6. For more information on telemedicine benefits and capabilities, see the American Telemedicine Association website, http://www.americantelemed.org/home. (Accessed June 14, 2018.)

7. Stanford Medicine 2017 Health Trends Report "Harnessing the Power of Data in Health," June 2017. https://med.stanford.edu/content/dam/sm/sm-news/documents/StanfordMedicineHealthTrendsWhitePaper2017.pdf. (Accessed June 14, 2018.)

8. This is commonly referred to as the B2C (or Business to Consumer) business model, as distinct from B2B (or Business to Business) model.

9. Wilson, Sonsini, Goodrich, and Rosati Digital Health Report, Fall 2017. https://www.wsgr.com/publications/PDFSearch/digital-health-report/Fall17/digital-health-report.htm. (Accessed June 14, 2018.)

10. Bruce Japsen, "AMA: Patients Responsible for 24 Percent of Medical Bill," *Forbes*, June 17, 2013. https://www.forbes.com/sites/brucejapsen/2013/06/17/ama-patients-responsible-for-24-percent-of-medical-bill/#2f9e7d4f34b0. (Accessed June 14, 2018.)

11. Health Maintenance Organizations provide health insurance plans that usually limit coverage to care from doctors who work for or contract with the HMO. Preferred Provider Organizations are a type of health plan that contracts with medical providers, such as hospitals and doctors, to create a network of participating providers. Health Savings Accounts are a type of savings account that allow the participant to set aside money on a pre-tax basis to pay for qualified medical expenses. For an excellent glossary of health care insurance related terminology, see https://www.healthcare.gov/glossary/. (Accessed June 14, 2018.)

12. For more discussion of these challenges, see George Lowenstein, et al. "Consumers' Misunderstanding of Health Insurance," *Journal of Health Economics* 32 (2013) 850–862. https://scholar.harvard.edu/laibson/publications/consumers-misunderstanding-health-insurance. (Accessed June 14, 2018.)

13. "How Engaged Are Consumers in Their Health and Health Care, and Why Does It Matter?" *Center for Studying Health System Change*, No. 8, October 2008. http://www.hschange.org/CONTENT/1019/. (Accessed June 14, 2018.)

14. "How Engaged Are Consumers in Their Health and Health Care, and Why Does It Matter?" *Center for Studying Health System Change,* No. 8, October 2008. http://www.hschange.org/CONTENT/1019/. (Accessed June 14, 2018.)

15. "How Engaged Are Consumers in Their Health and Health Care, and Why Does It Matter?" *Center for Studying Health System Change,* No. 8, October 2008. http://www.hschange.org/CONTENT/1019/. (Accessed June 14, 2018.)

16. "Only About 1 in 10 Adult Americans Have All the Skills Needed to Manage Their Health," *AHRQ News and Numbers*, May 14, 2008 AHRQ News and Numbers, Agency for Healthcare Research and Quality, Rockville, MD. Percentages add to more than 100% due to rounding. https://archive.ahrq.gov/research/jul08/0708RA41.htm. (Accessed June 14, 2018.)

17. For further discussion, see Tu, Ha T., "Surprising Decline in Consumers Seeking Health Information," *Center for the Study of Health Systems Change*, Tracking Report No. 26, November 2011. http://www.hschange.org/CONTENT/1260/1260.pdf. (Accessed June 14, 2018.)

18. For the complete study, see https://news.aetna.com/2015/04/survey-finds-americans-health-literacy-lacking/. (Accessed June 14, 2018.)

19. For the full Deloitte report, see https://www2.deloitte.com/content/dam/Deloitte/us/Documents/life-sciences-health-care/us-dchs-consumer-engagement-healthcare.pdf. (Accessed June 14, 2018.)

20. For a more detailed discussion, see Meera Viswanathan, PhD, "Interventions to Improve Adherence to Self-administered Medications for Chronic Diseases in the United States: A Systematic Review," *Annals of Internal Medicine*, December 2,

2012. http://annals.org/aim/fullarticle/1357338/interventions-improve-adherence-self-administered-medications-chronic-diseases-united-states. (Accessed June 14, 2018.)

21. 1.65E12 in "normal" notation 1,650,000,000,000 data points.
22. Richard Suskind and Daniel Suskind, *The Future of the Professions*. Oxford: Oxford University Press, 2015, p. 151.
23. For more discussion of this topic see Gienna Shaw, "Patients Don't Trust Information Technology," FierceHealthCare, January 5, 2017. https://www.fiercehealthcare.com/it/patients-don-t-trust-health-information-technology. (Accessed June 14, 2018.)

Chapter 5

Measuring Returns from Health Care IT Investments

5.1 Introduction

Information technology (IT) investments have often been proposed in an effort to improve the quality of health care services. Major milestones along this path include:

- The 1991 publication of The Institute of Medicine's *The Computer-Based Patient Record: An Essential Technology for Health Care*[1]
- George Bush's 2004 executive order creating a sub-cabinet position focusing on health care information technology, at which time he commented, "Within 10 years, every American must have a personal electronic medical record"[2] and
- The 2009 Health Information Technology for Economic and Clinical Health (HITECH) Act, enacted as part of the American Recovery and Reinvestment Act of 2009,

designed in part to promote the adoption and meaningful
use of health information technology using federal government financial incentives[3]

With this level of visibility and even funding, one might
expect that almost thirty years after the IOM's report, information technology investments would be commonplace and
evidence as to their efficacy in positively impacting patient
outcomes would be universal. Unfortunately, that is not the
case. This is due in part to the inherent challenges of successfully implementing information technology solutions generally,
and in part to the complexity of the health care environment
more specifically. While substantial IT investments have been
made in health care organizations, judgments about how successful they have been—particularly with improving patient
outcomes—remain inconclusive.

5.2 Importance of Productivity and Return on Investment

Economists have historically focused on determining value
from investments through measures of increased productivity. In other words, the value returned from an investment,
whether in buildings, people, tools, or IT has historically been
measured to the extent that it enhances the productivity of the
workers involved.

Chapter 2 described the challenges of measuring productivity in the services sector, and the relevance of these challenges
for health care as a services-based industry. But in health care,
the range of expected value from information technology
investments covers more than enhanced productivity, encom-
passing expectations of value coming from enhanced patient
safety, higher quality of clinical interventions, cost savings
and cost avoidance, and overall patient and provider satisfaction. Given the challenges scholars have had with productivity

measurements in general (and particularly in services industries), this much more extensive set of expected value creation
in health care raises the value bar significantly.[4]

Calculating the Return on Investment (ROI) from health
care information technology investments is a topic much
discussed in health care IT circles.[5] In many cases, the push
to calculate an ROI comes from those with backgrounds in
business—e.g., CFOs within a health care organization contemplating a significant investment in IT, or Boards of Trustees
whose members come from the business community and are
accustomed to making decisions based on the calculations of
financial returns from investments.

In highly simplified form, if you construct a building, then
rent out space in the building, the ROI is straightforward:

$$ROI = Annualized\,Rental\,Income$$
$$-\left(Amortized\,Construction\,Cost + Annual\,Maintenance\right)$$

If the result is a positive number that meets a certain thresh-
old, the decision is considered "a rational business decision."
The measurement of each of the terms in this equation is in
monetary form, so the calculation is both quantitative and
straightforward. Investors typically look for a minimum annual
return of 15%, although the range can increase to 40%–50% in
some circumstances.[6]

Unfortunately, information technology investments do not
fit such a simple model. In fact, what is represented here
as "Rental Income"—the recurring financial return from the
investment—becomes much less precise and less quantifi-
able with information technology investments in the health
care industry. How do you quantify the enhanced quality of
a service? How do you quantify estimated cost savings several
years into the future from service enhancements? What is the
value attributed to improved clinician and patient satisfaction?
How do you measure the avoidance of future costs that an IT
investment is expected to deliver?

Health care-specific challenges to realizing value from IT investments occur within the broader context of measuring the value realized from IT investments in general. The next section presents that context and along with it, notes how this adds complexity to considerations for health care IT investments.

5.3 Calculating the Value of Information Technology Investments

Determining the value of IT investments has always been a challenge. In large measure this is because such investments are most appropriately labeled as "complementary" investments in which value comes not so much from what the asset does on its own but from what it *complements* or what it *enables* other investments to achieve. Economists define "complementary assets" as those that require an additional investment, or "complement," to generate value for the organization.[7] For example, purchasing a computer and setting it on a desk generates little value; value begins, for example, when spreadsheet software is installed, and a worker then uses it to analyze financial data or when word processing software is installed and a worker can create electronic documents. *In a real sense, we can say that information technology in and of itself has no value; it is only in how the technology is used that value is generated.*

Stated more formally, it is only in *use* that technology investments generate value. In health care, acquiring and even implementing electronic medical record software, for example, does not in itself generate value; it is only when that software is used "in a meaningful way" that value is created.[8]

If information technology investments are considered "complementary," what other conditions or circumstances are necessary to generate—and measure—the value they produce? Organizational scholars and economists have offered guidance on these points. Alfred Chandler's classic work on *Strategy and Structure,*[9] for example, was followed by other books and articles that highlighted the importance of the interrelationships among several factors: strategy, organizational structure, employees, and technology.[10] In other words, IT investments by themselves offer little or no value unless coupled with other changes in organizational life, including strategy, structure, and worker skills.

Erik Brynjolfsson and his colleagues have been looking into these questions since the early 1990s. His observations are best summarized in the following comments:

> Our central argument is twofold: first, that a significant component of the failure of information technology is its ability to enable complementary organizational investments such as business processes and work practices; second, these investments in turn, lead to productivity increases by reducing costs and, more importantly, by enabling firms to increase output quality in the form of new products or in improvements in intangible aspects of existing products like convenience, timeliness, quality and variety.[11]

McKinsey & Company's research echoes much of what Brynjolfsson found by noting that to be effective, IT investments must be:

Tailored to sector-specific business processes and linked to performance levers
Deployed in a sequence that builds capabilities over time, and
Co-evolved with managerial and technical innovation [emphasis added][12]

"Tailored," "sequence," and "co-evolved with innovation" are key terms here. Without these types of complementary changes, it is unlikely that information technology investment will return measurable value to the organization. This is similar to the comment often attributed (but never specifically cited) to management guru Peter Drucker, that "Culture eats strategy for lunch." In other words, the culture of an organization—the beliefs, values, and norms that determine employee behaviors—has a significantly greater impact on an organization's ability to adapt to changing circumstances—including IT investments—than any formal strategy. Another saying is that "Bad processes overwhelm good products," which emphasizes that even the best product innovations (e.g., software) can be undermined if implemented while allowing bad processes to continue.

While little research to date has focused explicitly on measuring the value from information technology investments in the health care industry, there are findings on how such investments function in the world outside of health care. In these efforts, the point is made repeatedly that determining the value of IT investments in any industry is a challenge. Purchasing hardware and software, difficult and expensive as it may be, is the "easy part." Putting hardware and software to use is the "hard part," but also where the value lies. In fact, it is in the changes that are made in other aspects of a business that often determine whether an IT investment is a success or a failure. As the author of a non-health care case study noted, "Reaping the elusive productivity rewards of information technology requires that an organization must change the way it does business."[13]

But health care organizations, and especially hospitals, are particularly resistant to change regardless of whether such change is needed in management processes to complement IT investments or whether such changes are needed on their own to bring improvements in operational processes and policy.

The health care industry is a large and significantly bureaucratic industry. With collective revenues in the trillions, hundreds of thousands of employees, and a large number of specialized supporting organizations, it is truly a behemoth among industries in our economy. All of this creates resistance to change and an inertia that thwarts innovation at seemingly every turn. It also creates a mentality best stated as, "we can wait this out … and then get back to business as usual."[14]

A dismal picture of the success and failure of IT projects is noted in the fact that across industries, close to 40% of IT projects—and some claim as high as 70%—including new implementations and upgrades, are either stopped short of completion or when completed, fail to meet the goals established at the outset. Project plans typically lay out schedules for completion (time), financial goals to be managed (cost), and expectations as to what the project involves (scope). There is a saying that of time, cost, and scope, pick any two and the third will be out of control. In other words, projects managed to meet strict budget and time expectations will likely require changes in scope; managing to scope and budget will likely extend the time frame for the project; and managing to strict scope and time requirements may result in budget increases.[15]

IT investments in health care have followed trends in IT investments in other industries—with special challenges arising from health care's emphasis on "services" (noted in Chapter 2), the inherent risk adversity of physicians (noted in Chapter 3) and the overall resistance that the health care industry presents when confronted with opportunities to improve processes and technologies.

5.4 Major Phases of Information Technology Investments

IT investments, regardless of industry, have historically followed a path through three defined phases:

1. Substitution of technology for labor
2. Enhancement of labor productivity, and
3. Investments to improve the quality of an organization's product or service offering[16]

We divert briefly here from our health care focus to look at these phases, with attention to the content of each phase, the sequence of the phases, and the increasing complexity of measuring value that comes with each successive phase.

5.4.1 Phase 1: Labor Substitution

When computers are introduced into almost any organization, they are typically focused initially on automating manual tasks. Thus, economists talk about "substituting capital for labor" since the computers represent a capital investment and when they are installed the organization may be able to perform the same tasks as previously, but with fewer workers.

In health care, posting charges and billing tasks have historically been performed by financial clerks. But with the introduction of computers and software for financial management, manual tasks in areas such as budgeting and expense management and forecasting and later software for Admission, Discharge and Transfer (ADT) and patient accounting applications became automated. As illustrated earlier in Figure 2.3, these were among the earliest IT investments in health care. As a result, the need for staff resources diminished. When computers were introduced into ancillary departments such as Radiology, Clinical Laboratories, Pathology, and Pharmacy, the pattern was repeated; automating the tasks of inventory control and task scheduling required fewer staff, and technology continued to be substituted for labor. Measuring the value of these investments was relatively straightforward: computers came in and staff left, and it could be readily determined that the annual savings from staff reductions could easily exceed even the amortized cost of the IT investment.

5.4.2 Phase 2: Productivity Enhancement

Over the past two decades economists have been particularly interested in the relationship between information technology investments and productivity—the major relationship used to determine value.[17] This interest became a focused area of research when data from the 1980s and 1990s suggested that there was a *decrease* in U.S. labor productivity at a time when investments in information technology across industries were increasing.[18]

In general, growth in U.S. labor productivity during the post-World War II period had been averaging close to 3% per year until the early 1970s, when the average increase dropped to around 1.4% per year. This relatively low level of annual increases continued for two decades from the mid-1970s to the mid-1990s, when it began to increase at a rate of about 2.5% per year through the year 2000.[19] At the same time, "The rate of nominal business investment in information technology surged to 17% per year, from its 1987–1995 rate of 9%." The juxtaposition of these two rates—one decreasing and the other increasing quite dramatically—became known as a "productivity paradox."[20] If the purpose of information technology investments was to increase productivity, why were the industry data showing that productivity had decreased even with significant increases in information technology investments?

Two explanations are typically offered for this apparent paradox:

1. There is a "time lag" effect to IT investments—the "payoff" from the investment would typically take longer than with other types of investments so it would take some time for worker productivity to increase after the IT investments were made.
2. IT investments on their own were not sufficient to generate increases in productivity unless changes in workflow and processes (the complementary changes noted earlier) were changed to take advantage of the information technology investment.[21]

These two observations provided differentiating characteristics for information technology investments that began to set them apart from other types of investments such as buildings, manufacturing tools and techniques, and other technologies in which the return occurred both more quickly and with less dependence on "complementary" investments.

It was noted earlier that the measurement of productivity has historically focused on industry sectors in which the "inputs" and the "outputs" of an organizational process are well defined. Productivity is essentially a measure of efficiency: how many "input units" does it take to produce a specific "output unit"? To the extent that more output units are produced per input unit, a process can be said to be more "productive." In the manufacture of automobiles, for example, the input units are well defined (i.e., steel, plastic, rubber, aluminum, factory workers, machine tools, etc.). The finished output, an automobile, is similarly well defined. As a rule, then, the more automobiles that can be built with a given level of input resources, the more productive is the manufacturing process. One can then develop a financial model using the known costs of the input units and work through various pricing options for the finished product to provide a margin that satisfies whatever criteria of "success" is deemed appropriate by various stakeholders, including company executives, plant managers, bankers, stockholders, dealers, and customers.

Given the ability to quantify input resources in manufacturing, it is no surprise that economists interested in productivity have historically focused on manufacturing industries for the development of productivity measures. From the earlier discussion in Chapter 2 about the challenges inherent in measuring the quality of health care services, it is easy to understand why measuring changes in processes (which are somewhat akin to manufacturing) has become more of a focus than attempting to measure changes in patient outcomes.

But productivity does not always focus only on efficiency. In a narrow sense, one can be more "productive" creating more outputs with fewer inputs, but if the created product does not attain some identifiable standard of quality or performance, then this definition of "productivity" is too limited. Adding the notion that an output must achieve certain qualitative standards to be successful means that productivity must be judged not only on standards of efficiency but on the quality of the outcomes—a particularly problematic challenge in health care. Adding the expectation of effectiveness to productivity measurements for efficiency contributes significant additional challenges, particularly for services industries like health care in which outcomes are hard to define and measure.

Chapter 2 noted several of the fundamental differences between creating products and delivering services. These differences carry over to the challenge of measuring productivity. The measurement of productivity in the services sector of our economy has always been problematic and not much progress has been made over the past several decades, even as the services sector has grown significantly overall while manufacturing has decreased.[22] A now classic article published in the early 1980s noted the challenges similar to what was identified earlier in Chapter 2:

> The growth of the services economy presents special challenges for productivity analysts; output is often difficult to quantify, and measurement of labor input requires great care.[23]

With the challenges to defining inputs and outputs in services industries generally, attempting to identify the specific contribution of information technology investments to productivity in the services sector adds another level of complexity.

The health care sector does include a substantial number of jobs for which productivity measures focusing on inputs and outputs can be identified. Thus, the productivity of medical records staff who code charts can be measured, for example, by the number of charts coded in a day. Similarly, the productivity of housekeeping staff who clean and prepare patient rooms is amenable to measurement (e.g., how many rooms of which type can be cleaned in a day). But the accuracy of the coding and the cleanliness standards of housekeeping staff would still need to be considered.

On the other hand, the most expensive resources in health care (i.e., doctors, nurses, and other clinicians) are not engaged in work processes that can be measured (i.e., quantified) readily. While the cost of a physician's or nurse's time (the input) can be measured accurately, the output cannot. In part this is because: (1) they are providing services and not contributing to the creation of products;[24] and (2) the unit of output, improved health of the patient, is extraordinarily difficult to capture and may take years to be realized.

Until more specific definitions and measures of patient health status (which is the essence of what "quality" means in health care) can be established, our efforts to measure productivity in the health care sector will continue to rely on imperfect measures such as the pricing of inputs (e.g., drugs, procedures, lab tests, x-rays, etc.) and on the measurement of processes (e.g., patient days in the hospital, physician visits, etc.).

With all the challenges of measuring productivity in the health care sector generally, not only because it is a services-based industry, but because the outputs themselves are so challenging to measure, capturing the contribution of information technology to enhanced productivity in this sector has been and remains, elusive.

5.4.3 Phase 3: Improving Quality and Creating New Products and/or Services

Phase 3 of the information technology investment process focuses on improving the quality of products or services offered as well as the creation of new products and services which are enabled by information technology. As Brynjolfsson and Hitt have noted,

In today's economy, value depends increasingly on
product quality, timeliness, customization, conve-
nience, variety, and other intangibles.[25]

Many of the most successful "enabling" information technology investments have been in the field of communications. From
telegraphs to telephones, from wired to wireless, from main-
frames to mobile devices, the list of improvements in our ability
to collect, manage, analyze, and share data is simply staggering.
And while some of us do complain from time to time about the
need to interact with all these capabilities, much of what we do
today—especially in health care—would not have been possible without the technology investments that have been made in
improving the communication of information.[26]

In Phase 3, limitations on the measurement of services
quality become even more evident. Since the value from Phase
3 IT investments relies on improving quality and creating new
services, health care as an industry will continue to face serious measurement challenges.

It is important to recognize that as with the two previous phases of information technology investment (Labor
Substitution and Productivity Enhancement), the measurement
of value in the third phase is not only distinct but difficult.
Measurement in this phase does not focus on replacing people
with computers; nor does it attempt to make workers in any
industry necessarily more productive. Rather the intent is to
invest with the goal of both improving the quality of the work
or service being provided and/or to identify new products
that without an information technology investment, would not
exist. The challenge in health care is with the uniqueness of
a services industry, coupled with the roles of physicians and
patients, improvements in quality can be difficult to measure
(as noted in Chapter 2) and new services specifically enabled
by IT investments may be hard to identify. While service
processes may be made more efficient with the introduction of computerization, it remains problematic to determine

whether the process improvements will result in better patient outcomes.

Information technology investments have literally changed the lives of almost everyone. As noted earlier, this has much to do with the fact that information technology investments generate value that comes not directly from the investment itself, but rather from opening new opportunities and facilitating (and often requiring) complementary innovations.

In Phase 3, we begin to see the cumulative effects of investments made in the first two phases. Many organizations—working with a smaller work force due to reductions made in the first phase of their information technology investments and increases in productivity from Phase 2 investments—continue building on those foundations while focusing on improvements in the quality of the products they make and the services they provide. Having been successful in the initial two phases, they continue moving forward.

As organizations pass through each successive phase, it becomes increasingly more difficult to measure the specific gains to be achieved in the succeeding phase—both complexity and measurement challenges increase. Figure 5.1 highlights these changes from one phase to the next.

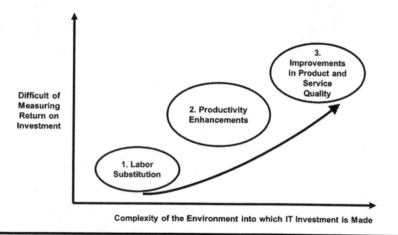

Figure 5.1 **Relationship between ROI measurement difficulty and environment complexity for each phase of IT investment.**

5.5 Summary

As IT investments are made in each successive phase, the environment into which these investments are made increases in complexity. Replacing staff with automated processes, as in Phase 1, can be relatively straightforward, since in this phase the investment is taking advantage of what computers do best: automating structured tasks that were previously performed by humans. One might assume that once staff have departed and computers are in place, the environment would become simpler. But in Phase 2, figuring out how to enhance productivity with fewer staff and more computers, becomes more difficult as easier options have already been exercised in Phase 1.

With Phase 2 investments the relationship between the IT investment and the human worker becomes more complex. Productivity enhancements are about workers' improving the amount of work they can complete with a given set of inputs. For example, having access to data electronically instead of relying on paper records generally saves a worker time and should enable that worker to do more work. But setting up databases that are accessible and relevant to a particular set of tasks in a services environment is a more complex undertaking than simply automating a set of specific, structured tasks and capturing the transactions in a database for later reporting. Also, at this stage with health care-specific electronic capabilities there is the increased risk that comes from managing access authorizations and protecting patient data from unauthorized use.

Phase 3 investments raise the level of complexity further. Value in this phase comes from the development of new strategies, new business processes and workflows, and possibly even new organizational structures—all designed to leverage IT investments to improve service and quality. However, health care organizations in general are not very good at embracing change. Value in this phase also comes from the interaction between system features, functions, and workflow into which the IT is inserted—a particularly difficult situation when physicians and patients are the focus. A major challenge in this phase is that organizational change in any industry, but especially in health care, can be time consuming, risky, costly, and benefits are likely to take time to accrue.

The three major phases of IT investments apply across all industries, including health care, although the path and timetable from one phase to the next may differ. Phase 1 investments in health care saw many of the same "substituting computers for people" process as happened in other industries—lower level staff were phased out as financial, billing, and departmental systems were introduced. Phase 2 investments focusing on productivity enhancements—particularly for Knowledge Workers—are harder to document in health care due to the challenge of measuring the productivity of Knowledge Workers and the services they provide. Phase 3 investments in health care have led to a variety of new service offerings and capabilities such as patient portals and telemedicine, although it is still unclear whether these bring the value that has been anticipated. At best, we can say that the progress of health care from one IT investment phase to the next has been uneven and uncertain and has resulted in a more complex combination of computers and people than is found in other industries.

At the 2017 Health Care Analytics Summit, more than 1,100 attendees were surveyed regarding their assessment of the success of the federal government's stimulus program for Electronic Health Records (EHRs) investment—essentially asking whether the investment in EHRs has been "worth it." The consensus seemed to be that the billions of dollars that the federal government had invested (not to mention the likely other billions of dollars that provider organizations have invested on their own) have generated less than stellar results. When asked to assess the success of the EHR incentives and the resulting implementations,

61% answered either "terrible" (19%) or "poor" (42%).

29% stated that the ROI from EHR investments has been "mediocre."

10% rated the ROI from EHRs as either "positive" (9%) or "superb" (1%).[27]

The combination of factors discussed in Chapters 1, 2, and 3 have contributed to these unfavorable assessments. One cannot imagine a more challenging set of factors for an IT investment: the combination of a services business, highly intelligent Knowledge Workers who are most comfortable with a significant amount of autonomy and resistant to change, working in an unstructured environment with customers who are themselves challenged to become engaged in the services process, all of which takes place within an industry that is itself reluctant to change. Perhaps it is somewhat understandable that not only is it challenging to bring IT investments into this mix but then attempting to measure the value or return from this investment is a situation not found in any other industry. All of this continues to build the case that health care as an industry is indeed the most complex in our economy.

Notes

1. Institute of Medicine, *The Computer-Based Patient Record: An Essential Technology for Health Care,* Revised Edition Washington, DC: The National Academies Press. https:// doi.org/10.17226/5306. (Accessed on June 16, 2018.) Report released initially in 1991.
2. "Bush Launches 10-Year-Effort To Create National EMR System," Managed Care News, June 1, 2004. https://www.managed-caremag.com/archives/2004/6/bush-launches-10-year-effort-create-national-emr-system. (Accessed on June 16, 2018.)
3. "HITECH Act Enforcement Interim Final Rule," https://www.hhs.gov/hipaa/for-professionals/special-topics/hitech-act-enforcement-interim-final-rule/index.html. (Accessed on June 16, 2018.)

4. Bill Conerly, "Productivity and Economic Growth," Forbes.com, May 19, 2015. https://www.forbes.com/sites/billconerly/2015/05/19/productivity-and-economic-growth/#6d6cf8195417. (Accessed on June 16, 2018.)

5. See, for example, Pam Arlotto and Jim Oakes, *Return on Investment: Maximizing the Value of Healthcare Information Technology* (Chicago: Healthcare Information Management Systems Society, 2003) and Pam Arlotto, et al., *Beyond Return on Investment: Expanding the Value of Healthcare Information Technology* (Chicago: Healthcare Information Management Systems Society, 2007).

6. Susan Schreter, "What's a Successful Return on Investment?" FoxBusiness.com, March 23, 2016. http://www.foxbusiness.com/features/whats-a-successful-return-on-investment. (Accessed on June 16, 2018.)

7. For an excellent discussion of complementary assets, see Alan Hughes and Michael S. Scott Morton, "The Transforming Power of Complementary Assets," *MIT Sloan Management Review*, Summer 2006 Research Feature, July 01, 2006. https://sloanreview.mit.edu/article/the-transforming-power-of-complementary-assets/. (Accessed on June 16, 2018.)

8. Our word play on the federal government's Meaningful Use initiative is intentional here. Regardless of how controversial and imperfect one may find the measures of Meaningful Use, the fact is the value of EMRs is not in their creation or even their implementation, but in how they are actually used, which is what the government is trying to measure.

9. A. D. Chandler, *Strategy and Structure*. Cambridge, MA: MIT Press, 1962.

10. In addition to Chandler's work, other important references would include H. J. Leavitt, *Managerial Psychology* (Chicago: University of Chicago Press, 1967), M.S. Scott Morton, *The Corporation of the 1990s: Information Technology and Organizational Transformation* (Oxford: Oxford University Press, 1990), T. Malone and J. Rockart, "Computers, Networks and the Corporation," *Scientific American* 6, no. 3 (March 1991), https://www.scientificamerican.com/magazine/sa/1991/09-01/ (accessed on June 16, 2018), and A. D. Chandler Jr. and J. W. Cortada, eds., *A National Transformed by Information: How Information has Shaped the United States from Colonial Times to the Present* (New York: Oxford University Press, 2000),

cited in Alan Hughes and Michael S. Scott Morton, "The Transforming Power of Complementary Assets," *MIT Sloan Management Review* 47, no. 4, Summer 2006. https://sloanreview.mit.edu/article/the-transforming-power-of-complementary-assets/. (Accessed on June 16, 2018.)

11. Erik Brynjolfsson and Lorin M. Hitt, "Beyond Computation: Information Technology, Organizational Transformation and Business Performance" *Journal of Economic Perspectives* 14, no. 4, Fall 2000, pp. 24–25. http://ebusiness.mit.edu/erik/Beyond%20Computation%20-%20JEP.pdf. (Accessed on June 16, 2018.)

12. Although somewhat dated, the findings and observations from this McKinsey & Co report are worth reviewing periodically since they are as relevant today as they were over 15 years ago. McKinsey & Co, *How IT Enables Productivity Growth: The U.S. Experience Across Three Sectors in the 1990s* (San Francisco: McKinsey & Co, 2002). https://www.mckinsey.com/business-functions/digital-mckinsey/our-insights/how-it-enables-productivity-growth. (Accessed on June 16, 2018.)

13. Hughes, Alan and Michael S. Scott Morton, "The Transforming Power of Complementary Assets," *MIT Sloan Management Review,* Summer 2006. https://sloanreview.mit.edu/article/the-transforming-power-of-complementary-assets/. (Accessed on June 16, 2018.)

14. Roy Smyth, "Why Changing Health Care Is So Hard," *Forbes*, February 24, 2014. https://www.forbes.com/sites/roysmythe/2014/02/24/why-changing-health-care-is-hard/#1930b1714f1b. (Accessed on June 16, 2018.)

15. "Health IT Success and Failure: Recommendations from Literature and an AMIA Workshop," *J Am Med Inform Assoc.* 2009 May–June; 16, no. 3, pp. 291–299, cited in https://www.ncbi.nlm.nih.gov/pmc/articles/PMC2732244/. (Accessed on June 16, 2018.)

16. Much of this discussion draws on earlier research by the author, some of which was published in "Finding Value from IT Investments: Exploring the Elusive ROI in Healthcare," *Journal of Healthcare Information Management* 17, no. 4, pp. 20–28. This article received HIMSS' Article of the Year Award in 2003. http://www.himss.org/finding-value-it-investments-exploring-elusive-roi-healthcare-jhim. (Accessed on June 16, 2018.)

17. The measurement of annual increases in productivity is important because the cumulative impact of even small increases in annual productivity can become huge over time—in short, the

rule of compound interest applies here. For example, a 1.5% annual increase in productivity will yield an overall cumulative increase of a little over 35% over a twenty-year period. If the annual increase goes up only slightly to 2.7% per year, over that same twenty-year period the cumulative increase will grow to 70%, or double what could be achieved with only a slightly smaller annual rate. Some economists would argue that since productivity increases over time enable "more to be done with less," productivity increases are one of the most important engines of overall economic growth in any society.

18. K. J. Stiroh, "Investing in Information Technology: Productivity Payoffs for U.S. Industries." *Current Issues in Economics and Finance*, Federal Reserve Bank of New York, June 2001, 7, no. 1. https://papers.ssrn.com/sol3/papers.cfm?abstract_id=702573. (Accessed on June 16, 2018.)

19. McKinsey Global Institute. U.S. Productivity Growth 1995–2000, *Understanding the Contribution of Information Technology Relative to Other Factors*, October 2001. https://www.mckinsey.com/~/media/McKinsey/Business%20Functions/McKinsey%20Digital/Our%20Insights/How%20IT%20enables%20productivity%20growth/MGI_How_IT_enables_productivity_report.ashx. (Accessed on June 16, 2018.)

20. Robert Solow, *The New York Times Book Review*, July 12, 1987. http://standupeconomist.com/solows-computer-age-quote-a-definitive-citation/. (Accessed on June 16, 2018.)

21. Eric Brynjolfsson and Lorin Hitt, "Beyond the Productivity Paradox: Computers Are the Catalyst for Bigger Change." *Communications of the ACM* 41, August 1998, no. 8. http://citeseerx.ist.psu.edu/viewdoc/summary?doi=10.1.1.195.1657. (Accessed on June 16, 2018.)

22. A review of data from the Bureau of Economic Analysis National Income and Product Accounts indicates that in the early post WWII years, private sector employment was split about 50/50 between "services" and "goods." By the end of the first decade of the twenty-first century, however, the split was over 80% devoted to "services" and less than 20% to "goods." We noted these changes in Chapter 2.

23. Jerome A. Mark, "Measurement of Productivity in Service Industries," *Monthly Labor Review*, June 1982. https://stats.bls.gov/opub/mlr/1982/06/art1full.pdf. (Accessed on June 16, 2018.) For a more recent effort to look at productivity in the

services sector, see Xiaofeng Li and David Prescott, "Measuring Productivity in the Services Sector," Canadian Tourism Human Resources Council, March 27, 2009. http://cthrc.ca/~/media/Files/CTHRC/Home/research_publications/productivity/Measuring_Productivity_Service_SectorSept_EN.ashx. (Accessed on June 16, 2018.)

24. See, for example, the discussion in Chapter 3.
25. Eric Brynjolfsson, E., and Lorin Hitt, "Beyond the Productivity Paradox: Computers Are the Catalyst for Bigger Change," *Communications of the ACM*, August 1998, 41, no. 8. http://citeseerx.ist.psu.edu/viewdoc/summary?doi=10.1.1.195.1657. (Accessed on June 16, 2018.)
26. As we noted in Chapter 4, collecting and storing data is the easy part; analyzing what it means remains incredibly difficult.
27. Health Catalyst, "Survey: Healthcare Technology Pros See Poor ROI from Electronic Records but View Analytics as a Solution," September 14, 2017. http://www.prnewswire.com/news-releases/survey-healthcare-technology-pros-see-poor-roi-from-electronic-records-but-view-analytics-as-a-solution-300519772.html. (Accessed on June 16, 2018.)

Chapter 6

Increasing Complexity of Medicine

6.1 Introduction

In previous chapters, we reviewed several factors that contribute to the complexity of the health care industry. These included:

- A look at how health care, as a "services-based" business differs in important ways from a "product-based" business (Chapter 2).
- An overview of the unique role physicians play in the health care industry (Chapter 3).
- A review of the challenges of working with patients who often don't participate in, or in many cases even understand, their own health challenges (Chapter 4).
- The difficulties of formally measuring returns from health care IT investments and making judgments about the quality of the services provided in the health care industry (Chapter 5).

In this chapter, we discuss several issues which impact the entire field of medicine, creating an overall level of complexity that on its own rivals that found in any other industry. We cover themes related to:

1. The increasing complexity of decision-making in the field of medicine, impacted both by an increase in *volume* of data that clinicians must work with and by the new *types* of data that come from areas such as genomics
2. The challenges of integrating research and clinical practice
3. Challenges that come from the burdens of regulation by the government and by professional associations

6.2 The Explosion of Data: Volume and Complexity

The amount of data available to a clinician for diagnostic and treatment purposes has increased dramatically over the past few years. Medline®[1] citations, for example, have grown from the approximately 160,000 that were added in 1964 to the almost 830,000 added in 2015,[2] with about half of these representing citations to articles published in the United States.

The amount of data that clinicians generate each time they see a patient is relatively small—typically less than 400kb per patient, which over time can grow to about 200 pages of text for a typical medical record. More extensive data can be added from imaging data. A full body PET scan, for example, can contain 9PB of data; a cardiac CT scan can grow to 36GB, and a functional MRI can include over 300GB of data.

The total amount of clinical data currently being created within health care overall is difficult to estimate accurately. However, a recent report provides some "ballpark" estimates, noting that as of 2013, there could be as much as

153 exabytes[3] of health care data in the world today, potentially increasing on an annual basis by as much as 48%:

> At the projected growth rate, [the amount of data in 2013] will swell to 2,314 Exabytes by 2020. To paint a picture, the authors of the report suggest storing all of that patient data on a stack of tablet computers. By the 2013 tally, that stack would reach nearly 5,500 miles high. Seven years later, that tower would grow to more than 82,000 miles high, bringing you more than a third of the way to the moon.[4]

There is perhaps no better example of the health care data explosion than what has resulted from the sequencing of human genomes:

> The sequencing machines that run today produce a million times more data than the machine used in the Human Genome Project [in 2003], and the Sanger Institute [now] produces more sequences in one hour than it did in its first 10 years.
>
> [Beyond the sequencing process itself] a single cancer genome project sequences data that requires up to 10,000 computer processing hours for analysis, and the Sanger Institute is doing tens of thousands of these at once. The sheer scale is enormous, and the computational effort required is huge.[5]

Figure 6.1 illustrates the extraordinary reductions in the cost of sequencing genomic data over the past decade, directly fueling the amount of data generated by sequencing activities. The chart illustrates that the declining costs of sequencing have outpaced the increased capabilities of computer chips.[6]

What is missing from the chart is the corresponding increase in the cost of collecting, managing, storing, analyzing, and other associated costs of attempting to use the results of

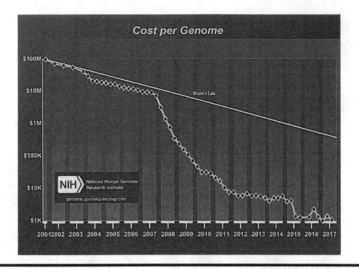

Figure 6.1 Reductions in the cost of human genome sequencing, 2001–2017. (From: "DNA Sequencing Costs: Data," https://www. genome.gov/sequencingcostsdata/. Accessed June 16, 2018.)

sequencing data. The cost components often missing from the straightforward sequencing estimates include:

> [Q]uality assessment/control, … technology development to improve sequencing pipelines, development of bioinformatics/computational tools to improve sequencing pipelines or to improve downstream sequence analysis, management of individual sequencing projects, informatics equipment, and data analysis downstream of initial data processing (for example, sequence assembly, sequence alignments, identifying variants and interpretation of results).[7]

Figure 6.2 illustrates this point.

Beyond the challenge of keeping up with the sheer amount of data related to health care generally (including both clinical care and sequencing), a clinician today is also faced with ever greater levels of complexity in the data itself—particularly as genomic data has become increasingly relevant and important to patient diagnosis and treatment.

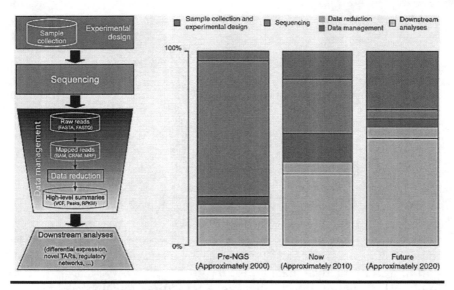

Figure 6.2 Shifts in costs from sequencing to downstream analyses. (From: Andrea Sboner, et al., "The real cost of sequencing: higher than you think!" *Genome Biology* 2011, 12:125, https://genomebiology.biomedcentral.com/articles/10.1186/gb-2011-12-8-125. Accessed June 16, 2018.)

Dr. Bill Stead, Chief Strategy Officer at Vanderbilt University Medical Center, Nashville, has developed an iconic representation of the challenges faced by clinicians in reaching diagnostic and therapeutic decisions about their patients by observing that the data sets available for decision-making are likely to increase exponentially over time[8] (see Figure 6.3).

For the most part, observations about a patient's *phenotype* have historically been used to inform a clinician's decision-making, including the determination of disease and as the basis for a recommended treatment. When a patient's *genotype* starts to be considered, the amount of data to be reviewed on behalf of a patient increases significantly.[9] With the advent of "genomic" medicine in which the patient's genomic expression patterns enter the analysis, and genomic medicine probes deeper into structures and pathways of cells literally at the molecular level, the number of facts needed to reach a decision escalates significantly.

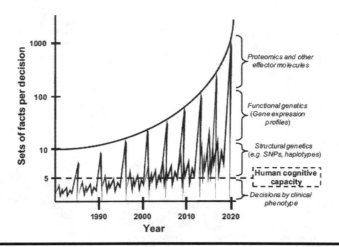

Figure 6.3 Comparison of human cognitive capacity with the explosion of new biomedical data types. (From: Stead, W. W.; Searle, J. R.; Fessler, H. E.; Smith, J. W.; Shortliffe, E. H. "Biomedical Informatics: Changing What Physicians Need to Know and How They Learn," *Academic Medicine* 2011, 86(4):429–434. Accessed on June 17, 2018. Used with permission.)

Supporting Dr. Stead's observation is this recent comment from the *New England Journal of Medicine*:

> Medical knowledge is expanding rapidly, with a widening array of therapies and diagnostics fueled by advances in immunology, genetics, and systems biology. Patients are older, with more coexisting illnesses and more medications. They see more specialists and undergo more diagnostic testing, which leads to exponential accumulation of electronic health record (EHR) data. Every patient is now a "big data" challenge, with vast amounts of information on past trajectories and current states. All this information strains our collective ability to think. Medical decision-making has become maddeningly complex.[10]

As biomedical knowledge in general is enhanced more and more by discoveries from fields such as genomics, and as the amount of data generated by imaging studies continues to grow as well, the individual clinician's ability to process this knowledge and apply it at the point of care, becomes more and more difficult.

Another source of both volume and complexity stems from the rapid increase in new laboratory testing capabilities. As illustrated in Figure 6.4, over the past two decades, the growth in number of unique laboratory tests has expanded exponentially, while the number of laboratories performing those tests has remained relatively constant. In other words, even with a constant supply of testing facilities, the amount of information available from new tests has increased substantially. Direct to consumer testing, in which consumers rather than clinicians submit specimens for laboratory analysis and receive the

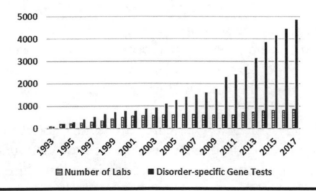

Figure 6.4   Growth in numbers of labs and gene-specific laboratory tests. (Data for this chart was originally sourced from the government funded genetests.org website. Unfortunately, this site was taken down effective 12/1/2017, with the rationale that there were other sites that were collecting the same data but had better access tools. At the time of its closure, the site contained data on more than 68,000 genetic tests, 5,000 inherited disorders, 6,000 genes, 700 labs, and 1,000 clinics. For more information, see https://www.genomeweb.com/ molecular-diagnostics/longstanding-genetic-testing-website-genetests-closing#.WuIpm4jwbIU. Accessed June 16, 2018.)

results directly, is estimated to grow from $15 million annually in 2010 to $350 million in 2020.[11]

Clayton Christensen has provided some insight into this challenge by identifying three major stages of medical practice which represent a path to improve the processing of medical knowledge, particularly with the increasing use of ever more specific understandings of disease, treatment, and outcomes. Christensen distinguishes these stages as follows:

Intuitive medicine – care for conditions can be diagnosed only by their symptoms and only treated with therapies whose efficacy is uncertain. By its very nature, intuitive medicine depends upon the skill and judgment of capable but costly physicians.

Empirical medicine – occurs when a field has progressed into an era of "pattern recognition"—when correlations between actions and outcomes are consistent enough that results can be predicted in probabilistic terms.

Precision medicine – the provision of care for diseases which can be precisely diagnosed, whose causes are understood, and which consequently can be treated with rules-based therapies that are predictably effective.[12]

Historically much of what clinicians know about medicine has been acquired "intuitively," based on the accumulated knowledge and experience of the clinician at the time of the encounter with the patient. However, as medical knowledge has progressed and the efficacy of certain interventions can be demonstrated, we expect to move along the continuum to clinical practice based more on empirically validated results—precision medicine.

The transition from "intuitive" to "precision" medicine will be a difficult and challenging process, in part because, as Jerome Groopman has argued, physicians approach their work in ways similar to most of us and can make similar errors in judgment.[13] These include patterns of "attribution," "cognition" and "availability."[14] The challenge is to recognize these patterns, their strengths and weaknesses, and then incorporate the ability to learn from the increasing amounts of data that is becoming available.

On the down side, as the type, number and size of available data sources grow, we can expect much overlap and conflicting information to occur—and as a result more challenges to the transition from intuitive to precision medicine. Absent strict management of terminology (which is the current situation), one physician's description of a patient's illness may not match another's, even though the underlying illness may be the same. (This challenge is discussed in more detail in Chapter 7.) The ability to query vast amounts of data, even assuming that the definitions of data elements are standardized, becomes not only difficult, but impossible in some cases. Simply put, decision-making in many areas of medicine is becoming much more complex due in part to the explosion of data now being collected and made available to physicians.

As one commentator has noted,

> Medical thinking has become vastly more complex, mirroring changes in our patients, our health care system, and medical science. The complexity of medicine now exceeds the capacity of the human mind.[15]

One cannot imagine anything described here occurring in the absence of electronic computing capabilities. On the other hand, we are also seeing that the creation of new computational capabilities and the expectations that come with them, stretches the abilities of organizations to respond. Information Technology (IT) departments in hospitals, for example, have historically focused on managing computing hardware and communications on a scale significantly less than what is now required by the explosion in data volume and user expectations that have accompanied innovations in images and genome sequencing.

It is easy to forget that at least a portion of the large volumes of the data being collected, managed and stored must from time to time be moved from one location to another. This can require substantially new communications capabilities quite beyond the relatively simple task of sending of data messages from one system to another. Even the customary running of computer updates overnight in many facilities has become problematic as large-scale data transfers compete for scarce communications resources.

As medicine continues to develop new capabilities, including new understandings of disease origins and new treatment regimens, the relationships among data elements will continue to become more complex. This data complexity does not come so much from adding data similar to what has been collected historically as it does from the discovery of entirely new data structures and content. This in turn brings new relationships among data elements that, as they are discovered or defined, add to existing sets of data. This process becomes a never-ending upward spiral of more data, more data relationships, different data, new relationships—and more complexity. None of this would be possible without IT investments.

6.3 Big Data and Analytics

The discussion about patients and information technology would be incomplete without noting two "buzz words" that seem to dominate when talking about the collection and management of patient data in health care: "big data" and "analytics."

Data collection is exploding in every industry, and health care is no exception. With the advent of electronic medical records over the past 20 years, there are now thousands of data repositories of clinical data—every electronic medical record (EMR) implementation typically has at least two: (1) A "production" database in which the clinical data that is

collected on a daily basis is stored, and (2) a "data repository" or "data warehouse" which is optimized for ad hoc and
routine reports. Because of the requirements for clinicians'
immediate access to clinical data it is important for this data
to be unencumbered by ad hoc queries or the generation
of reports that might affect the performance of the production database. Therefore, most organizations create a separate
database which is populated periodically with copies of production data. Data from other sources such as laboratory and
pharmacy systems may be added to create a "data repository"
or "data warehouse." As this repository/warehouse expands,
portions of specialized data may be extracted and copied into
"data lakes" or "data marts"—specialized extracts of data from
larger repositories—to enable reports and queries to run with
optimal efficiency.[16]

There do not appear to be any universally accepted definitions of what "big data" is. However, SAS, the large statistical
software company, has developed a useful definition which
describes five important dimensions of "big data": volume,
velocity, variety, variability, and complexity.[17]

The data collected during the process of a patient's encounters with his or her physician, when added to imaging and
genomic data, would seem to conform to these dimensions.
In addition, the content of patient data can change rapidly,
from one visit to the next, or in some cases from one day to
the next if a patient's condition is improving or deteriorating
rapidly. The variety of data collected across an episode of care
can be extensive and highly variable. And of course, as we
have been discussing throughout, collecting and managing
data on the human experience leads to extraordinarily complex data structures and content.

Note that volume is only one dimension of "big data"; the
other attributes are of equal importance and distinguish what
otherwise could be a standard database. Volume, velocity, variety, variability and complexity are all attributes of clinical data
generally. In fact, one might argue that clinical data is likely

on the high end of these attributes when compared with the levels of variability and complexity found in the databases of other industries.

As the data in production databases, repositories, lakes and marts continues to accumulate, the question arises: is there value in such a large asset that can extracted for the benefit of the organization? As these storehouses of data grow, the challenge shifts from collecting and managing the data to the task of finding out what it means—hence the "analytics" challenge.

Three challenges make the analysis of health care data especially difficult:

Unstructured data – much of the data in today's clinical databases is unstructured. Doctor's notes, even when following the POMR (problem-oriented medical record) and SOAP (subjective, objective, assessment, and plan) protocols discussed later in Chapter 7, for example, typically do not conform to any formal data model, and when entered as textual data may be heavily dependent on an individual clinician's preferred way of describing the activity being documented.

Lack of standardization – The lack of standardized terminology for describing health-related events is discussed extensively in Chapter 7. This undermines significantly the ability to extract value from "big data" in health care. If multiple terminologies are used to describe what is essentially the same situation, then drawing conclusions from the data becomes problematic.

Context – Often a specific data element cannot be clearly understood unless a context is provided: when, where, why, and how that data element was collected. A specific term, for example, may have high importance in some situations but much less in others. Capturing context is a difficult challenge for computers since contextual descriptions may range from a single adjective to a much larger phrase to an entire sentence or paragraph.

Clinical data sources in health care are diverse and often incompatible; standards development has been ongoing for close to 50 years, with acceptance and implementation still a challenge[18]. When analytics identifies trends from clinical "big data" repositories, the next challenge is to translate these findings into the diagnostic and treatment workflow of clinicians, who are often resistant to change.[19]

There are, however, some important success stories on the use of big data. Consider the following:

deCode, a genetics discovery company located in Reykjavik, Iceland, has over the past 20+ years, collected genotypic and medical data from well over half of the adult population of Iceland. Using this genetic data in combination with medical records data, deCode has put together a genealogy database covering not only Iceland's current population but has been able to establish genetic relationships stretching back to the founding of the country more than 1,000 years ago. Interestingly, the company struggled to find a market for this data and the linkages they uncovered until it was acquired in 2012 by Amgen, a large American biotechnology/drug development company. Historically about 90% of Amgen's drug candidates have failed to make it to the market. Amgen now tests three-quarters of its candidate drugs against the deCode data and in the process is expected to significantly reduce its historical failure rate by testing against relationships found in the deCode database.[20]

FlatIron Health, a start-up focused on the collection of vast quantities of data on cancer patients (now claiming that they have data on 20% of all cancer patients in the U.S.), has focused on the big data challenges by developing a human curation process for the data it receives from health centers across the country. FlatIron discovered that about half of the data they were collecting was in unstructured form—pathology reports, clinical reports, etc.[21] Flatiron's value added selling point, ironically, came through humans. With unstructured data, it takes human reviewers to discover and understand context, which can challenge a computer algorithm on its own. After the data has been collected, it is reviewed by humans who "clean" the data (also known as curation) by identifying structure and context. As noted by Dr. Amy Abernethy, FlatIron's Chief Medical Officer, "The real challenge isn't to gather the data, but to clean it up, ... And that's really hard without an understanding of context."[22]

Express Scripts administers 1.4 billion prescriptions for 100 million Americans each year. When patients don't take the medications or fail to refill them, the costs can be upward of $100 billion annually, stemming largely from the complications that patients suffer from gaps in taking their medications. Express Scripts has a huge patient database from which they have been able to extract 300 factors that helps in understanding why patients do not fill or refill a prescription. By assigning risk scores to patients, and then initiating follow-up, Express Scripts has been able to reduce nonadherence by close to 40%, which clearly benefits patients and the company.[23]

It is difficult for stand-alone facilities like hospitals and physicians' offices to collect and manage sufficient data to enter the realm of "big data" and "analytics." Even health systems comprised of many individual hospitals and physician practices may be challenged because of the problems of interoperability among systems in different locations—even when these systems are provided by common vendors. (This problem is discussed in more detail in Chapter 7.) However, disruptive changes such as mergers between retail drugstore chains (many of which already provide health care through urgent care centers or on-site clinics) and insurance companies may provide new opportunities for the emergence of big data and analytics' capabilities.[24]

The path from big data to improved patient outcomes is a circuitous one. Data repositories whether from deCode, FlatIron or Express Scripts, are filled with historical data, which they continue to accumulate at a rapid rate. While correlations among data elements can be helpful, one must proceed cautiously. For example, patients with X disease and Y outcome who have a Z genetic defect may be an interesting correlation, but until we understand more about how that particular genetic defect impacts either the disease or the outcome we are not likely to see specific impacts on patient care. Correlations such as these may help to pinpoint possible new causal relationships, although some correlations may also turn out to be specious since there may be an intervening event or pathway that the correlation overlooks. However, big data can provide an excellent starting point for knowledge development and point the way to further inquiry and refinement in how the data are collected and analyzed as well as enhancing our understanding of why a particular correlation seems to work at all.

6.4 Increasing Integration of Research and Clinical Practice

Research and clinical practice have historically been separate domains: research was practiced in university settings, while clinical practice occurred in hospitals and physicians' offices. In recent years, however, the boundaries between these arenas have been going away as new approaches such as "clinical research," "research-driven practice" and "translational research" have become more common. In addition, patients (especially those with life-threatening illnesses) are unwilling to wait an estimated seventeen years for the results from research to make their way into clinical practice.[25] While there has been much progress in lowering this approximately "two decade" time frame, the organizational separation between where research is carried out and where clinical care is delivered continues to present barriers to moving as quickly as possible from scientific discovery to improved clinical outcomes.

In addition, there are significant concerns about the validity of some of the published articles and the clinical practices they engender, and concerns about the underlying accuracy of some of the scientific data on which new knowledge has been generated and shared. These can be challenges to our ability to determine what is "true" and what it not. Even today, it is estimated between 30% and 60% of the genomic data currently stored in the federal government's Genbank may be erroneous.[26] In addition, the track record of published research leading to improved clinical practice is itself challenged by what appear to be research efforts that have turned out to be at best a mislabeling of data sources or, at worst, outright fraudulent.

The explosion of medical journals in recent years has also contributed to the problem—particularly those with little or no formal "peer review" process. Omics International, a company based in India, claims over 1,000 open access journals which collectively post 50,000 articles in fields such as medicine, technology, and engineering, typically without engaging in the formal "peer review" process which has historically been standard practice with professional journals.[27]

In one of the larger known cases of academic misconduct, an anesthesiologist was accused of fabricating data and then publishing almost two dozen articles using the false data—articles which in some cases purported to change clinical practice.[28]

The National Cancer Institute (NCI) makes available to cancer researchers cell lines which have been cultured in the laboratory and shared to stimulate further research. However, several years ago it was discovered that one of the NCI's 60 published cell lines, labeled as "breast cancer," was actually an ovarian tumor cell line, and as many as 300 papers may have been published with the incorrect identification.[29]

Beyond the challenge of outright fraudulent research and apparent specimen mis-labeling, there is a more serious trend with research data now labeled as the "reproducibility crisis." Whether in psychology, artificial intelligence, or cancer research, scientists are discovering that it is not only difficult but at times impossible to replicate the published findings of their peers.[30]

Kevin Coombes and Keith Baggerly, two statisticians at The University of Texas MD Anderson Cancer Center, effectively created a new field called "forensic bioinformatics" after they attempted to reproduce the results of a major cancer study conducted at Duke University first reported in the *New England Journal of Medicine* and later in *Nature*—two of the premier peer-reviewed journals in the field of medicine.[31] The statisticians uncovered an inevitable "can of worms" after they identified numerous errors in the reported data. The fallout from Baggerly's and Coombes' work was extensive: the journal articles authored by the Duke researchers were retracted, formal investigations were undertaken by both Duke and the Institute of Medicine, clinical trials which were based on the research were cancelled, the lead researcher (who was subsequently discovered to have falsified his background and academic credentials) resigned, CBS' *60 Minutes* aired a segment on "Deception at Duke,"[32] and a malpractice lawsuit was filed on behalf of the patients who had been enrolled in the clinical trials.[33]

With this as background, it is not surprising that the task of processing biomedical knowledge to arrive at a diagnostic or therapeutic decision is a significant challenge in itself. Likely, no other field is faced with such obstacles to clarity and direction. Nevertheless, this is the context in which clinicians meet with patients every day, gather data on symptoms, review data from tests their patients have received, and move ahead not only with a diagnosis but in most cases, with a recommended treatment regimen.

It is not sufficient that a new drug may be found in the laboratory to be efficacious in the treatment of a disease and subsequently lead to changes in clinical practice; challenges come from all the attendant collateral processes that need to be developed, including dosage parameters, identification, and management of possible adverse reactions in some patients, educational materials, training of clinicians in the use of the new drug, etc. We need to get to the point that what was research data yesterday, becomes clinical data today, and the basis for predictive models for diagnosis and treatment tomorrow. This process (outlined in Figure 6.5) is circular, and once we can measure patient outcomes in a meaningful way,[34] this data becomes the basis for further scientific inquiry and discovery.[35]

While the steps above are well laid out, it is the velocity with which the circle is moving that determines the actual time frame from discovery to care. Under the heading of "Using Information Technology," the Agency for Healthcare Quality and Research (AHRQ) has made this observation:

> The potential for technology to translate research findings into sustainable health care improvements has long been recognized. Technology may be utilized to accelerate the implementation of research throughout organizations more rapidly than would occur if translation strategies depended on individuals or personal interactions.[36]

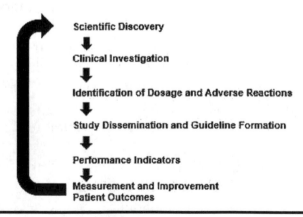

Figure 6.5 Steps from scientific discovery to influencing patient outcomes.

Although the arrows in Figure 6.5 indicate a singular right-hand circulation, the process of scientific discovery in the "real world" is not so uniform. In fact, the arrows circulate both ways: integration of research and clinical data can be improved by incorporating what we are learning through scientific discovery and, as well, scientific discovery processes can be improved by linking them more closely with clinical outcomes. The mechanism for making these linkages possible is the data itself: using data from scientific discovery processes to improve clinical care, and in turn using data on clinical outcomes to pose questions which might be able to be tested through scientific research processes.

One of major efforts to establish and validate the efficacy of clinical interventions has been supported by the Cochrane Collaboration, which uses close to 21,000 members organized into review groups in more than 100 countries.[37] In a recent report on the conclusions from over a thousand reviews, it was determined in 49% of the cases the evidence did not support either benefit or harm, and in 96% of the cases, more research was recommended.[38] In short, it would appear about half the time clinicians continue to practice in the realm of "intuitive medicine," and we have a ways to go until medicine is more empirically based, and a long ways to go before clinicians are practicing "precision" medicine.[39] For those asking whether medicine is being practiced as an art or a science, the documentation suggests we are still very much on the side of art.

Yet another barrier to crossing the divide between research and clinical practice lies in the privacy and security provisions of the Health Information Privacy and Accountability Act (HIPAA).[40] (The challenges from HIPAA are discussed in more detail in Chapter 8). When research is based on clinical data (or collected specimens), there are significant restrictions on who can access that data and the circumstances under which it can be accessed and used. Electronic medical record (EMR) data, for example, cannot simply be "repurposed" for research without establishing that the data has been "de-identified" or "anonymized," or that the patient whose data is being sought has given explicit and written consent for its use in specific research projects. As EMRs retain increasing amounts of patient clinical data, the subsequent use of that data for research (so-called secondary uses which differ from the primary purpose of collecting the data for clinical diagnosis and treatment) can be an opportunity to improve clinical outcomes—assuming, of course, that the patient has given permission for such use.

To assure that health care organizations manage appropriately the rights of their patients over the use of their data, they are required to establish institutional review boards (IRBs),

> authorized under FDA regulations, to review and monitor biomedical research involving human subjects. ... [A]n IRB has the authority to approve, require modifications in (to secure approval), or disapprove research. This group review serves an important role in the protection of the rights and welfare of human research subjects.[41]

Another approach to managing the barriers between research and clinical interests has been the development of "honest brokers." These are individuals or organizations that are accepted as "neutral parties" responsible for protecting the rights of patients in the use of their data (or specimens) and at the same time acknowledging the legitimacy of using patient data (or specimens) for research purposes.[42]

The integration of research and clinical practice is extraordinarily complex on its own, since it can take place both informally as well as more formally through IRBs, honest broker requests, or in the move from chance observations and intuition to structured clinical trials. Unfortunately, this approach relies more often on a "random event" process than one that has been created for predictable outcomes. So, the challenge becomes how to create access to data sources and relationships—"clinical" as well as "research"—so that some of the "randomness" is taken out of the discovery process, in effect placing much less reliance on AHRQ's "individuals or personal interactions." There are several specific tasks which need to be defined and implemented to accomplish this:

■ Letting clinicians and investigators know what data is being stored and where the data is located;
■ Standardizing terminology and vocabulary in general so semantic challenges are minimized;
■ Recognizing and protecting the rights of patients regarding how their data is being used.

Integrating research into clinical practice is one of the major mechanisms for the improvement of clinical care. Introducing IT capabilities into this process is one way to both structure events more clearly and develop appropriate pathways for clinicians to follow in replicating the published results of the research community.

6.5 Burden of Regulation: Government and Professional

Anyone who works anywhere in the health care system can attest to the overriding, and some might feel overbearing, influence of regulators. This is true for hospital administrators managing the delivery of health care services, physicians delivering those services, pharmaceutical executives planning the development of new drugs, pharmacists dispensing those drugs, medical directors making coverage decisions for health maintenance organizations, and even computer consultants planning a medical website. Outsiders, both in the government and in private accrediting and certifying organizations, have a major role in telling health care workers at all levels what to do.[43]

Many industries feel burdened by regulations imposed at the federal, state and local levels. Among these are regulations regarding employment, worker safety, taxes, the environment, intellectual property and consumer protection, etc. Yet it can be argued that the health care industry, particularly on the provider side, is more heavily regulated than any private business because not only must it function under the regulatory oversight that every other industry faces, but in addition, it must operate under numerous health care-specific regulations and requirements from professional associations.

Most industries face regulatory compliance from the following Federal agencies[44]:

- Environmental Protection Agency (EPA)
- Occupational Safety and Health Administration (OSHA)
- United States Department of Agriculture (USDA)
- Department of Defense (DOD)
- Department of Homeland Security (DHS)
- Department of Justice (DOJ)
- Department of Labor (DOL)
- Federal Trade Commission (FTC)
- Internal Revenue Service (IRS)

In the health care industry, however, there are additional federal agencies with regulatory authority which focus specifically on health care. Within the Department of Health and Human Services (DHHS), for example, these include:

- Agency for Healthcare Research and Quality (AHRQ)
- Centers for Disease Control and Prevention (CDC)
- Centers for Medicare and Medicaid Services (CMS)
- Food and Drug Administration (FDA)

- Health Resources and Services Administration (HRSA)
- Indian Health Services (IHS)
- National Institutes of Health (NIH)
- Substance Abuse and Mental Health Services Administration (SAMHSA)
- Office for Civil Rights (OCR)
- Office of Inspector General (OIG)

At the state level, there are regulatory departments that have oversight for health care, and in many localities, there are departments that exercise similar regulatory roles:

- Departments of Health (State and Local)
- Boards of Medicine Licensing
- Licensing Boards for Allied Health Professionals
- Departments of Welfare
- Departments of Insurance

In addition to the myriad of public agencies regulating health care, there are private professional organizations which have authority over the licensing of health care organizations and the professionals who work in the field:

- Accreditation Council on Graduate Medical Education (ACGME)
- American Board of Medical Specialties (ABMS)
- Association of Schools of Allied Health Professions (ASAHP)
- Education Commission for Foreign Medical Graduates (ECFMG)
- Federation of State Medical Boards (FSMB)
- Joint Commission on Accreditation of Healthcare Organizations (JCAHO)
- Liaison Committee on Medical Education (LCME)
- Medical specialty societies
- National Board of Medical Examiners (NBME)

- ■ National Committee on Quality Assurance (NCQA)
- ■ United Network for Organ Sharing (UNOS)

Beyond the regulatory agencies focused on both business in general and health care specifically, legislative mandates have both stimulated health care IT investment and challenged many areas of health care (including hospitals, health systems, long care facilities, ancillary health organizations and clinicians). Most recently, as we noted earlier, the HITECH legislation provided funding for the implementation of Electronic Medical Records (EMRs) while at the same time through requirements for demonstrating "meaningful use," stipulated penalties for those who chose not to make the investment or were not able to meet the standards for compliance.[45]

While providers and provider organizations are attempting to work successfully within this regulatory environment, they are also facing mandates to update the practices they use for coding the care they provide. The International Classification of Diseases (ICD) coding manual for inpatient diagnoses and procedures was initially developed in 1900, and by 1998 had gone through nine major revisions.[46] This version of the coding standard (ICD-9) contained over 20,000 code sets that became integral to clinical practice. However, in 2009 the federal government mandated that all health care organizations and providers upgrade to ICD Version 10, which increased the number of codes to over 155,000.[47] Coding a sprained ankle, for example, used 5 coding options in ICD-9; this increased to 45 in ICD-10. Angioplasty previously used only one code in ICD9; with ICD-10, the number of coding options increased to 1,170.[48]

A recent study reported that physicians currently spend over 20% of their time "interacting with insurers on formularies, claims, billing, credentialing, pre-authorizations, and quality measures data," a number which is certainly likely to increase,[49] with a concomitant increase in physician workload.

Companies working in the health care industry may not be affected by every regulatory agency or legislative mandate or even every regulation promulgated by federal, state, and local agencies. However, their customers—hospitals, payers, clinicians, managers—do feel the impact of all of this, must deal with this complex set of rules and regulations, and must consider them in the process of contemplating any investment, including IT.

Notes

1. MEDLINE® contains journal citations and abstracts for biomedical literature from around the world and is often consulted by clinicians seeking recent clinical developments. It's companion resource, PubMed®, provides free access to MEDLINE and links to full text articles if where possible. https://www.nlm.nih.gov/bsd/pmresources.html. (Accessed June 16, 2018.)
2. "MEDLINE® Citation Counts by Year of Publication," https://www.nlm.nih.gov/bsd/medline_cit_counts_yr_pub.html. (Accessed June 16, 2018.)
3. This amount of data is hard to imagine. It may be useful to recall the current nomenclature of data sizes: a byte is a single character; a kilobyte (KB) is 1,024 bytes; a megabyte (MB) is 1,024 kilobytes or about 800–900 pages of text; a gigabyte (GB) is 1,024 MB, or a movie at TV quality; a terabyte (TB) is 1,024 GB or over 1,600 CDs or 4.5 million books; a petabyte (PB) is 1,024 GB is about 20 million 4-drawer filing cabinets; an Exabyte is 1,024 PB or about the amount of data created on the Internet each day in 2012 or 250 million DVDs. See https://www.zmescience.com/science/how-big-data-can-get/. (Accessed June 16, 2018.)
4. Kenneth Corbin, "How CIOs Can Prepare for Healthcare 'Data Tsunami'," *CIO*, December 16, 2014. https://www.cio.com/article/2860072/healthcare/how-cios-can-prepare-for-healthcare-data-tsunami.html. (Accessed June 16, 2018.) Note: Research firm IDC predicts an exponential increase in healthcare data, including data from new sources outside the control of IT. In response, CIOs need to prioritize compliance in governance policies and get a handle on "shadow IT."
5. Sophie Curtis, "Data-Driven Medicine: Understanding the Link between Genetics and Disease," *The Telegraph*, October 16, 2013. http://www.telegraph.co.uk/technology/news/10380095/

Data-driven-medicine-understanding-the-link-between-genetics-and-disease.html?goback=%2Egde_2181454_member_5796248969474486272#%21. (Accessed June 16, 2018.)

6. Moore's law is attributed to Gordon Moore, co-founder of Fairchild Semiconductor and Intel. In 1975, Moore postulated that the number of components per integrated circuit would double every two years, thus increasing computing capacity and driving down costs. As is evident in this graph, the decreasing costs of human genome sequencing have significantly outpaced Moore's law.

7. Andrea Sboner, et al., "The Real Cost of Sequencing: Higher Than You Think!" *Genome Biology* 2011, 12, no. 125, https://genomebiology.biomedcentral.com/articles/10.1186/gb-2011-12-8-125. (Accessed June 16, 2018.)

8. The graph in Figure 6.3 is intended to be descriptive at a high level and is not based on any actual analysis of how many data points enter any specific decision.

9. An organism's "phenotype" consists of all of the characteristics of the organism that are observable; its "genotype" is the set of genes carried by the organism.

10. Ziad Obermeyer, M.D., and Thomas H. Lee, M.D., "Lost in Thought—The Limits of the Human Mind and the Future of Medicine," Perspective, *The New England Journal of Medicine,* September 28, 2017. http://www.nejm.org/doi/full/10.1056/NEJMp1705348. (Accessed June 16, 2018.)

11. Stanford Medicine, "2017 Health Trends Report Harnessing the Power of Data in Health," Stanford University School of Medicine, June 2017. https://med.stanford.edu/content/dam/sm/sm-news/documents/StanfordMedicineHealthTrendsWhitePaper2017.pdf. (Accessed on June 13, 2018.)

12. Clayton Christensen, *The Innovator's Prescription.* New York: McGraw Hill, 2009, pp. 44–45.

13. Jerome Groopman, *How Doctors Think.* Melbourne: Scribe Publications, 2010.

14. "Attribution" errors reflect the tendency to explain someone's behavior based on internal factors, such as personality or disposition. "Cognitive" distortions convince us that something is true when in fact it isn't. "Availability" errors refer to problem of remembering one alternative outcome of a situation much more easily than another.

15. Ziad Obermeyer, M.D., and Thomas H. Lee, M.D., "Lost in Thought—The Limits of the Human Mind and the Future of Medicine," Perspective, *The New England Journal of Medicine*, September 28, 2017. http://www.nejm.org/doi/full/10.1056/NEJMp1705348. (Accessed June 16, 2018.)

16. A data repository or warehouse typically brings together a variety of data from disparate sources, which can then be used as the source for analytics and reports for the organization. A "data mart" (a subset of a data warehouse) is akin to a bottle of water ... "cleansed, packaged and structured for easy consumption while a data lake is more like a body of water in its natural state. Data flows from the streams (the source systems) to the lake. Users have access to the lake to examine, take samples or dive in." See https://www.blue-granite.com/blog/bid/402596/top-five-differences-between-data-lakes-and-data-warehouses. (Accessed June 16, 2018.)

17. "Big Data: What It Is and Why It Matters," https://www.sas.com/en_us/insights/big-data/what-is-big-data.html. (Accessed June 16, 2018.)

18. See Chapter 7, "Clinical Data Management and Sharing" for more discussion of this challenge.

19. See earlier discussions about physicians and industry resistance to change in Chapter 3.

20. Erika Fry and Sy Mukherjee, "Tech's Next Big Wave: Big Data Meets Biology," Fortune.com, March 19, 2018. http://fortune.com/2018/03/19/big-data-digital-health-tech/. (Accessed June 16, 2018.) Also Amgen Press Release, "Amgen to Acquire deCODE Genetics, a Global Leader in Human Genetics" http://investors.amgen.com/phoenix.zhtml?c=61656&p=irol-newsArticle&ID=1765710. (Accessed June 16, 2018.)

21. David, Shaywitz, "The Deeply Human Core of Roche's $2.1 Billion Tech Acquisition—And Why It Made It," Forbes.com, February 18, 2018. https://www.forbes.com/sites/davidshaywitz/2018/02/18/the-deeply-human-core-of-roches-2-1b-tech-acquisition-and-why-they-did-it/#4b2be75729c2. (Accessed June 16, 2018.)

22. Erika Fry and Sy Mukherjee, "Tech's Next Big Wave: Big Data Meets Biology," Fortune.com, March 19, 2018. http://fortune.com/2018/03/19/big-data-digital-health-tech. (Accessed June 16, 2018.)

23. Erika Fry and Sy Mukherjee, "Tech's Next Big Wave: Big Data Meets Biology," Fortune.com, March 19, 2018. http://fortune.com/2018/03/19/big-data-digital-health-tech. (Accessed June 16, 2018.)

24. See, for example, "Merger Medicine and the Disappearing Doctor," *The New York Times*, April 8, 2018. https://www.nytimes.com/2018/04/07/health/health-care-mergers-doctors.html?rref=collection%2Fsectioncollection%2Fbusiness&action=click&contentCollection=business&region=rank&module=package&version=highlights&contentPlacement=2&pgtype=sectionfront. (Accessed June 16, 2018.)

25. Zoe Slote Morris, et al., "The Answer Is 17 Years, What Is the Question: Understanding Time Lags in Translational Research," *Journal of the Royal Society of Medicine* 104, no. 12, December 2011. http://journals.sagepub.com/doi/abs/10.1258/jrsm.2011.110180. (Accessed June 16, 2018.)

26. See Hammer, Joachim and Markus Schneider, "Going Back to our Database Roots for Managing Genomic Data," *OMICS, A Journal of Integrative Biology* 7, no. 1, 2003, p. 117. https://www.liebertpub.com/doi/abs/10.1089/153623103322006751. (Accessed June 16, 2018.)

27. Esmé E Deprez and Caroline Chen, "Medical Journals Have a Fake News Problem," Bloomberg.com, August 29, 2017. https://www.bloomberg.com/news/features/2017-08-29/medical-journals-have-a-fake-news-problem. (Accessed June 16, 2018.)

28. "Fraud Case Stuns Anesthesiologists," *Anesthesiology News*, April 3, 2009. http://www.anesthesiologynews.com/ViewArticle.aspx?d_id=21&a_id=12868. (Accessed June 16, 2018.) Also reported in "Doctor Admits Pain Studies Were Fraudulent," *The New York Times*, March 11, 2009. https://www.nytimes.com/2009/03/11/health/research/11pain.html. (Accessed June 16, 2018.)

29. Iscovitch M, Ravid D., "A Case Study in Misidentification of Cancer Cell Lines: MCF-7/AdrR Cells (Re-Designated NCI/ADR-RES) Are Derived from OVCAR-8 Human Ovarian Carcinoma Cells," *Cancer Lett.* 2007 Jan 8;245(1-2):350-2. Epub February 28, 2006. https://www.ncbi.nlm.nih.gov/pubmed/16504380. (Accessed June 16, 2018.)

30. Christie, Aschwanden, "Failure Is Moving Science Forward," FiveThirtyEight, March 24, 2016. https://fivethirtyeight.com/features/failure-is-moving-science-forward/. (Accessed June 16, 2018.) See also, Matthew Hutson, "Missing Data

Hinder Replication of Artificial Intelligence Studies," *Science*, February 15, 2018. http://www.sciencemag.org/news/2018/02/missing-data-hinder-replication-artificial-intelligence-studies. (Accessed June 16, 2018.)

31. See "Misconduct in Science: An Array of Errors," *The Economist*, September 10, 2011. https://www.economist.com/node/21528593 (Accessed June 16, 2018.) See also Bob Carlson "Putting Oncology Patients at Risk," *Biotechnology Healthcare*. 2012 Fall; v. 9 no. 3, pp. 17–21. https://www.ncbi.nlm.nih.gov/pmc/articles/PMC3474449/. (Accessed June 16, 2018.)

32. "Deception at Duke: Fraud in Cancer Care?" https://www.cbsnews.com/news/deception-at-duke-fraud-in-cancer-care/. (Accessed June 16, 2018.)

33. Jay Price, "Trial on Anil Potti's (clinical) Trial Scandal Postponed Because Lawyers Get the Sniffles (updated)," errorstatistics.com, January 26, 2015. https://errorstatistics.com/2015/01/26/trial-on-anil-potti-trial-scandal-postponed-because-lawyers-get-the-sniffles-rejected-post/. (Accessed June 16, 2018.)

34. Note our earlier discussion in Chapter 6 regarding the difficulties in measuring the outcomes from treatment regimens.

35. Califf RM, Peterson ED, Gibbons RJ, Garson A Jr, Brindis RG, Beller GA, Smith SC Jr. Integrating quality into the cycle of therapeutic development. *J Am Coll Cardiol*. 2002; 40:1895–1901. https://www.ncbi.nlm.nih.gov/pubmed/12475447. (Accessed June 16, 2018.)

36. Agency for Healthcare Research and Quality, Translating Research into Practice (TRIP) II, (Washington, D.C.: AHRQ Pub. No. 01-P017 March 2001) p. 2. https://archive.ahrq.gov/research/findings/factsheets/translating/tripfac/trip2fac.html. (Accessed June 16, 2018.)

37. http://www.cochrane.org. (Accessed June 16, 2018.)

38. Regina P. El Dib, Álvaro N. Atallah, Regis B. Andriolo "Mapping the Cochrane evidence for decision making in health care," *Journal of Evaluation in Clinical Practice* 13 (2007), pp. 689–692. https://www.ncbi.nlm.nih.gov/pubmed/17683315. (Accessed June 16, 2018.)

39. The distinctions among intuitive medicine, empirically-based medicine and "precision" medicine are discussed extensively in Clayton Christensen's *The Innovator's Prescription*. New York: McGraw-Hill, 2009, pp. 44–45.

40. The Health Insurance Portability and Accountability Act of 1996 (HIPAA), Public Law 104-191, enacted standards for the electronic exchange, privacy and security of health information. This law and its implications for increasing the complexity of the health care industry is discussed in Chapter 8.

41. "Institutional Review Boards Frequently Asked Questions—Information Sheet," https://www.fda.gov/RegulatoryInformation/Guidances/ucm126420.htm. (Accessed June 16, 2018.)

42. Hyo Joung Choi, et al.,"Establishing the Role of Honest Broker: Bridging the Gap between Protecting Personal Health Data and Clinical Research Efficiency," *PeerJ.* 2015; 3: e1506. https://www.ncbi.nlm.nih.gov/pmc/articles/PMC4690386/. (Accessed June 16, 2018.)

43. Robert I. Field, *Healthcare Regulation in America: Complexity, Confrontation and Compromise.* New York: Oxford University Press, 2007, Preface.

44. This listing comes from Robert I. Field, op. cit., Appendix B.

45. 2009 Health Information Technology for Economic and Clinical Health Act (HITECH Act), https://www.hhs.gov/sites/default/files/ocr/privacy/hipaa/understanding/coveredentities/hitechact.pdf. (Accessed June 16, 2018.)

46. National Center for Health Statistics, Classification of Diseases, Functioning, and Disability. https://www.cdc.gov/nchs/icd/icd9.htm. (Accessed June 16, 2018.)

47. Statute and Regulations, ICD-10 Final Rule. https://www.cms.gov/Medicare/Coding/ICD10/Statute_Regulations.html. (Accessed June 16, 2018.)

48. "Why We Need 1,170 Codes for Angioplasty," *Wall Street Journal*, November 11, 2008. https://www.wsj.com/articles/SB122636897819516185. (Accessed June 16, 2018.)

49. Walker Ray, MD, and Tim Norbeck, "Healthcare Is Turning into An Industry Focused on Compliance, Regulation Rather Than Patient Care," Forbes.com, November 5, 2011. http://www.forbes.com/sites/physiciansfoundation/2013/11/05/healthcare-is-turing-into-an-industry-focused-on-compliance-regulation-rather-than-patient-care/. (Accessed June 16, 2018.)

Chapter 7

Clinical Data Management and Sharing

7.1 Introduction

When a patient visits a physician's office or is admitted to a hospital, the records from that visit have historically been retained in paper files either in the physician's office or in the hospital's medical records department. Several types of data may be collected or accessed during a visit or a hospital stay, including the physician's personal observations, a more formal history, and physical examination report, results from clinical labs, etc. Historically, the collection of patient data has suffered from three major issues:

1. The type and frequency of data collection depended largely on the individual physician's preferences, style, training and interest.
2. Since data collection was largely a manual process, the resulting hand-written notes often proved to be illegible not only to others who would have to review the notes in

the patient's medical record, but in some cases, even to the physician who wrote them initially.

3. A patient's data, collected and stored in a physician's office or in a hospital, was often unavailable if the patient saw a different doctor or was admitted to a different hospital.

7.2 Structuring Clinical Data

Several major developments in the last century have had a lasting impact on solving the first two issues mentioned above. First, the *Flexner Report*, published by the Carnegie Foundation in 1910, served as a major critique of the state of medical education at the time.[1] In addition to arguing that there were too many medical schools (many small and run as for-profits), the Report cited the lack of stringent admissions standards and the absence of a strong science-based curriculum. The Report also encouraged physicians to keep a patient-oriented medical record, building on the work of Dr. Henry Plummer and his colleagues at the Mayo Clinic who started what they called the "unit record" in which patient visits and other types of patient-specific information were collected and stored in a single folder.[2]

> Dr. Plummer introduced a centralized medical record consisting of a big envelope where all doctors would aggregate all the information regarding a particular patient. Each patient was assigned a unique identifier and his/her own dossier of clinical documents. The medical record would follow the patient everywhere at Mayo and all physicians would have access to all records.[3]
>
> … But Dr. Plummer did not stop at creating the patient centric comprehensive medical record. After

tinkering with a complex system of cables and pulleys, Dr. Plummer came up with a pneumatic system of tubes and conveyors to rush patient records from one office to another. He also invented a communication system between physicians in exam rooms based on the telephone system and a telegraph ticker.[4]

These were influential efforts in creating a formal "medical record" to replace the historically more common ledger-type of listing of patients seen and payments made.

But even with the recognition of the need for a formal patient medical record, it was not until almost fifty years later that structuring the content of that record became recognized as an essential component of documenting the patients' experience with their physician.

In 1968, Dr. Lawrence Weed published "Medical Records That Guide and Teach,"[5] an article that became one of the most widely cited in the field of medical informatics. As he noted in a 2014 interview:

> I realized then—and it was very upsetting—that they [students] weren't getting any of the discipline of scientific training on those wards, … When I pick up a chart that is a bunch of scribbles, I say: 'That's not art. It certainly isn't science. Now, God knows what it is.'[6]

In his article, Dr. Weed described two concepts that fundamentally changed the way that physicians document their encounters with patients:

1. **POMR** (Problem-Oriented Medical Record), which focuses the clinician's attention on the specific problems that are facing the patient.
2. **SOAP** (Subjective, Objective, Assessment and Plan), which is a structured process for documenting the

physician's experience with the patient. Although initially focused on physician documentation, SOAP is now used for most forms of clinical documentation and is especially helpful for enhancing the communication among teams of caregivers.

With Dr. Weed's contribution and its impact on medical documentation, significant progress was made toward resolving the first of the three challenges (structuring clinical documentation) identified earlier.

7.3 From Paper to Electronic Records

Paper-based medical records could be shared only to the extent that a clinician could go to an organization's medical record department and review the paper medical record, which likely contained lab results, radiology reports as well as the observations of other clinicians. Unfortunately, not only was this inefficient, but often ineffective as well. For example, physicians' notes were often hand written and famously illegible. In addition, the movement of medical record files from the medical records department to a clinical department (e.g., in anticipation of a patient appointment) meant that at times the patient's medical record was unavailable for review. Not infrequently, the medical record was "not available" since it became lost either in the manual re-filing process or during its transport around the organization.

In addition, clinical documentation of the care provided within a clinical department at times did not become a part of the patient's permanent medical record because the clinician taking care of the patient wanted to retain documentation within his/her own department. The result was the creation of "shadow files."

The implementation of Electronic Medical Records (EMRs) changed all of this. Paper records were considered "obsolete" as clinical documentation was increasingly captured electronically, and the patient's permanent medical record became an electronic document. Electronic documentation based on POMR and SOAP structures provided templates for physicians to use. In addition, hand-written notes were effectively eliminated as physician notes were entered directly into the EMR via a keyboard.

Prior to the implementation of enterprise EMRs, paper records often became "electronic" through large scale scanning operations. Unfortunately, the resulting electronic "picture" of the paper records were simply "snapshots" of paper documents and their content was not searchable even though scanned documents were in fact more widely available than paper records.

7.4 Electronic Medical Records

The third challenge (the inability to share information easily) has been met only in part by the introduction of both departmental and enterprise-wide electronic medical record capabilities.

The development of electronic systems supporting ancillary systems such as pathology and radiology brought significant improvements over the paper processes that initially supported these departmentally based activities. The availability of minicomputers enabled departments to purchase and implement their own computer systems quite independent of the mainframe systems that typically supported Admission, Discharge and Transfer (ADT) capabilities as well as patient billing and more general financial systems.[7] In many cases, these departmental systems provided more department-specific functionality than was available on enterprise-wide, mainframe-based systems. However, these departmental systems often used data structures and workflow more amenable to their own internal work processes than with sharing data (i.e., systems "interoperating" with each other) with other systems in the organization.

This problem was most acute in large provider settings such as hospitals in which patient data was collected from many sources and systems but needed to be shared or exchanged with other systems. For example, the data collected at the time of a patient's admission to the hospital, or when a patient is transferred to a different room (or discharged entirely) needs to be shared with the laboratory system to assure that orders for laboratory work result in the correct clinical results being available to the clinician. Similarly, medication orders sent to the pharmacy need patient location data to assure that drugs will be delivered to the right patient in the right room. Radiology systems have similar challenges—x-rays need patient data to ensure that the physician knows which patient's films are being reviewed. When patients are discharged, it is important that all these ancillary systems have this information as quickly as possible to avoid, for example, medications being sent to a patient room after the patient has left. It was not uncommon through the early 1970s for hospitals to have multiple data terminals at nursing stations to facilitate access to admissions data and ancillary data such as laboratory results.

Increasingly, records in both physicians' offices and hospitals are being kept in EMRs. The statistics for EMR adoptions show a dramatic increase over just the past few years. As of 2015:

- 87% of office-based physicians had adopted any EMR.
- 78% had adopted a certified EMR.
- 54% had adopted a basic EMR.

With regard to physician adoption of office-based systems, since 2008,

- Adoption in general increased from 42% to 87%.
- Adoption of basic EMRs more than tripled from 17% to 54%.

In 2015, 96% of all non-federal acute care hospitals possessed a certified EMR. Small rural and urban hospitals had the lowest rates at 94%, while large and medium hospitals were closer to 98%.[8]

One of the challenges to the sharing of patient data is that vendors selling into the health care provider market compete with each other, and do not have a strong financial incentive to develop the capability to share data with their competitor's products. In the market for hospital EMRs, for example, three vendors have close to 70% of the market, with the remainder shared by a number of smaller vendors.[9] On the ambulatory side, the vendor marketplace is highly fragmented—at the end of 2015, for example, there were over 680 vendors supplying "certified health care IT to ... ambulatory primary care physicians, medical and surgical specialists, podiatrists, optometrists, dentists, and chiropractors participating in the Medicare EHR Incentive Program."[10]

The essence of the relationship between the clinician and the patient has been captured historically in the patient's written medical record, and now electronically in the EMR. Although many IT investments have been labeled as "mission critical," few approach the criticality of EMRs for the patients as well as for the clinicians.[11] Systems in other industries typically characterized as "critical to the business mission" generally focus on financial risk, and do not carry the personal risk to patients associated with an EMR system that is not available or has been compromised at the time of the patient encounter with a clinician. Even with its criticality, EMRs are fraught with challenges from inconsistent terminology standards, are at risk for data breaches, and in general introduce inefficiencies into the clinical workflow they were designed to support and have become a burden on the clinicians who use them.

Chapter 3 discussed the challenges of providing effective and efficient—and ultimately helpful—information technology investments for physicians. A recent poll of over 500 primary care physicians (cited earlier) confirmed that EMRs still fall short of being considered a useful additional capability for the clinician.[12]

Overall there is a sense that even after close to 40 years of effort, software companies still have not provided information technology products that physicians find consistently useful in their work. Again, the complexity of health care is underscored with this data.

Electronic medical records occupy a place in the portfolio of health care information technology applications that is central not only to the clinical operations, but in some cases to the lives of the patients who receive care. The EMRs are the accumulation of every essential service transaction, drive the creation of almost every billing transaction, are the initiators of other services transactions (through electronic orders processing), and are the source of every service event that drives the provider side of the health care business. Few other industries have or reach this level of IT criticality, nor face the level of complexity that is found in health care.[13]

7.5 Interoperability

The challenge of sending data from a source system to a receiving system is not unique to health care. And in fact, early efforts with financial transactions such as sending purchase orders and receiving confirmation that the order had been received, provided a foundation for later work on interoperability standards in health care. What was especially valuable to the subsequent sharing of health-related data was the inclusion of components such as "query-response handling, acknowledgments and error handling" to provide assurance that not only was data sent, but that it was received with the same content that was sent initially.[14]

Successful efforts like the POMR and SOAP provide a structured framework within which clinicians can collect and organize the data they are gathering about their patients. These frameworks, however, do not address the actual sharing of patient data—the ability, for example, to take patient data collected in one setting and easily share it with another setting. If a patient is being seen by more than one physician, is referred to another physician for specialty care or goes to a facility for emergency or urgent care, the patient's medical history residing in one location may be highly relevant for whatever care needs to be provided either by a different physician or in a different facility. Without consistent and standardized terminology, individual physicians' use of POMR and SOAP may contain sufficient inconsistencies to limit the "sharability" of patient data.

If patients were seen by only one doctor during their lifetimes or were admitted to just one hospital, the need for medical records to be "interoperable" would be much less urgent. Consider these results from a recent survey:

■ Patients in general have seen an average of 18.7 different doctors during their lives.
■ Patients between the ages of 18 and 24 have seen an average of 8.3 doctors.
■ Patients over 65 years of age have seen an average of 28.4 individual doctors.
■ The average person has over a dozen medical record charts scattered around the country.
■ The average patient visit generates 13 pieces of paper.
■ The average paper medical chart weighs 1.5 lbs.[15]

Electronic Medical Record systems, by virtue of their electronic capabilities, should be able to facilitate the sharing of clinical data across organizational and clinical boundaries, in effect eliminating the barriers of hand-written documentation. But for this to happen, the collection and storage of clinical data in one location must be able to be accessed, available and "understood" in another setting. This is the essence of "interoperability":

> Interoperability describes the extent to which systems and devices can exchange data and interpret that shared data. For two systems to be interoperable, they must be able to exchange data and subsequently present that data such that it can be understood by a user.[16]

With regard to health care specifically,

> ... [I]nteroperability is the ability of different information technology systems and software applications to communicate, exchange data, and use the information that has been exchanged. Data exchange schema and standards should permit data to be shared across clinician, lab, hospital, pharmacy, and patient regardless of the application or application vendor.[17]

The lack of interoperability among EMR systems can have significant consequences for patients. As noted in one recent discussion:

> In the United States, there is no single format used by all providers, and hospitals have no incentive to make it easy to transfer records from one place to another. The medical records mess is hobbling research and impeding attempts to improve patient care.[18]

The process of collecting data across institutional boundaries can be expensive and frustrating. We noted in Chapter 6 that FlatIron Health, a start-up recently acquired by Roche, was able to assemble a database of close to 2.2 million records from cancer patients across the country, but in the process required the services of 900 nurses, certified tumor registrars and people with master's degrees in coding data—an effort well beyond the resources of any single hospital or health system. In Flat Iron's experience, some medical centers would not accept electronic patient signatures giving consent to share records; others simply ignored requests to share records, and when a paper record was provided for review, it could run to 100 or 200 pages, all of which had to be reviewed manually to collect the data needed for a specific project.[19]

Interoperability clearly still challenges us today—even with Dr. Weed's path-breaking work on the structuring of clinical data and with the promulgation of electronic medical record-keeping systems in place in many physician offices and hospitals. The next section reviews the evolution of standards intended to facilitate the transport and sharing of data *structures*, and then focuses on one of the major remaining challenges: the development of standards related to the *content* of clinical data.

7.6 Standards Development for Data Structures

The history of standards development in general dates back to the early 1900s when several electrical, mining and mechanical engineering professional associations formed an international body with the purpose of "establishing an impartial national body to coordinate standards development, approve national consensus standards, and halt user confusion on acceptability."[20] Their initial success in developing a standard for pipe threads, for example, led to later work focused on a variety of safety standards and codes across industries. The American Standards Association was formed from a variety of professional standards-setting groups in 1928, and in 1967 became the American National Standards Institute (ANSI). Along the way, what has evolved is a formal, structured discussion and voting process that eventually provided legitimacy for standards-setting in a variety of industries as well as the later work on interoperability standards in health care.

The development of standards for interoperability in health care began at the University of California at San Francisco (UCSF) in 1976 with a project led by Don Simborg, a physician and the first CIO at UCSF, working with Steve Tolchin from the Johns Hopkins University Applied Physics Laboratory (APL). Prior to joining UCSF, Dr. Simborg had worked at Johns Hopkins developing departmental solutions for radiology and pharmacy and had done some work with the APL.

The UCSF effort focused on the creation of "message standards," encapsulating essential data elements originating in one system (e.g., an admissions system) and then sending those standardized messages to a receiving system (e.g., a laboratory system) which would in return acknowledge acceptance of the message and use the data for its own purposes. These data standards operated at the application or 7th level of the OSI "stack" of communications standards which had been evolving over the previous decade.[21] Simborg's and Tolchin's work at UCSF was the first effort to develop an interoperability protocol at the Applications Level of the OSI model and became the foundation of the subsequent Health Level 7 (HL7) protocol.[22]

A somewhat similar effort on clinical data standards development was started in the late 1970s, led by Clem McDonald at the University of Indiana School of Medicine and Ed Hammond of the Division of Medical Informatics at Duke University. McDonald had written an editorial for an American Medical Association publication comparing the need to establish clinical data standards to the development of universal product codes (UPCs) in the grocery industry. UPCs were developed long before there was a practical use for them and McDonald argued that the medical professions should be doing the same.[23]

McDonald and Hammond and others worked through the American Society of Testing and Materials (ASTM) organization and established a subcommittee on "Standards for the Exchange of Clinical Data." The standard that was developed through this subcommittee became the "first published, balloted, consensus standard for clinical data."[24]

As Simborg worked to establish clinical interoperability standards based on his work at UCSF and later his StatLan commercial product, his company made the decision that the HL7 protocol needed to be released as an open rather than a proprietary protocol. Hence, he organized a meeting in March 1987 with the initial four StatLan customers (Moses Cone Hospital, Auburn Faith Community Hospital, Rochester General Hospital and the Hospital of the University of Pennsylvania) and several departmental system vendors who supported the StatLan protocol. The eventual result of these discussions was HL7v1, the first formal version of the Health Level 7 protocol, published in October 1987.[25]

While Simborg's and McDonald's efforts continued on somewhat parallel paths for several years, they and the membership of the HL7 and ASTM committees realized that evolving into a single organization would enable more efficient standards development processes. HL7v2 was released in 1990 and contained standards descriptions that were very similar to what the ASTM efforts had achieved, which further brought the two efforts closer together. In 1996, McDonald gave up his chairmanship of the ASTM Committee as part of an effort to bring the two processes together. Ironically the merging of these efforts was assisted significantly by the fact that McDonald had chaired both the HL7 and the ASTM efforts for several years.[26]

In 1996, HL7v2 became an ANSI-accredited health care standard which put the overall HL7 efforts on a national and eventually international stage of Standards Developing Organizations (SDOs). As of 2018, the HL7 organization had over 1,600 members in more than 50 countries, including over 500 corporate members representing "health care providers, government stakeholders, payers, pharmaceutical companies, vendors/suppliers, and consulting firms."[27] More than twenty years later, HL7v2 remains the dominant interoperability standard in the health care industry.

HL7v3 was released in 2005 and represented a fundamental shift in standards development. HL7v2 development has been influenced largely by clinical information specialists—the actual users of the interfaces, who felt that the value of the standard would increase as more sites and vendors adopted it. The development of HL7v3, on the other hand, was influenced largely by medical informaticists who felt that HL7v2 was too flexible, lacked a formal data model as well as well-defined application and user rules and in general needed to be more precise.[28]

Unfortunately, this new direction meant that HL7v3 was not backward compatible with HL7v2 as it essentially redefined the content of the HL7 standard. The focus shifted from making data interoperable through the use of messaging standards to the creation of a set of architecture and document standards based on a Reference Information Model (RIM) as well as specifications for data, document and vocabulary types.[29] The introduction of a Clinical Data Architecture (CDA) as well as specifications for a Continuity of Care Document (CCD) represented a significant departure from previous HL7v2 efforts. The successful implementation of HL7v3 requires fundamental changes not only in interoperability processes but in many cases in the data and document definitions, which vendors have been developing on their own over the past thirty years. Not surprisingly, to date actual HL7v3 implementations are few and HL7v2 continues to be the predominant standard for interoperability in the U.S. health care industry.[30]

The challenges and struggles of interoperability illustrated by HL7v2 and HL7v3 standards development processes have more recently led to a new standard, Fast Healthcare Interoperability Resources (FHIR). FHIR is best described as:

> ... a next generation standards framework created by HL7. FHIR combines the best features of HL7's v2, HL7 v3 and CDA product lines while leveraging the latest web standards and applying a tight focus on ease of implementation.[31]

FHIR seeks to overcome the obstacles created by the fundamental differences between HL7v2 and HL7v3 and the implementation challenges that came with HL7v3. FHIR accomplishes this by making implementation easier, leveraging web standards such as XML, JSON, HTTP, and OAuth, and focusing on making the exchange of information as seamless as possible. As the FHIR standard works its way through HL7's standards review process, the testing of current versions, the development of new versions and actual implementations are underway. It will take time (as with any new standard) to determine whether FHIR is the answer to many of the continuing challenges with interoperability, although early indications are that it holds much promise.

7.7 Standards Development for Data Content

As we have noted, the shift from HL7v2 to HL7v3 represented a fundamental change from standards focused on messages (i.e., the *structure* of data elements) that enable moving data from a source system to a recipient system (or multiple systems) to standards attempting to define the actual *content* of that data. The fact that more than a dozen years after HL7v3 was introduced there are still few actual implementations of the full suite of that version's products, underscores one of the most significant challenges remaining in clinical data management and sharing—the development of standards for the *content* of the data used by clinicians to describe the diagnosis and treatment of their patients. HL7v2 focused on the creation of structural standards to enable the *transport* of clinical data from one location to another; it did not address the problem of *content* or "meaning"—how to assure that the terms that a clinician uses in one setting can be understood easily by a clinician in another setting.

The distinction between structure and content is best described by noting the differences between synoptic interoperability and semantic interoperability:

Synoptic interoperability refers to the package in which data elements are encapsulated. HL7v2 is an example of a synoptic interoperability standard in that it defines standards for messages sent from one computer system to another.

Semantic interoperability refers to the ability of data elements in one computer system to be used in another computer system with no ambiguity as to the meaning or content of the initial use. Semantic interoperability in many cases must include the context of the initial use since data elements can take on different meanings depending on what surrounds them.

Another way to distinguish between synoptic and semantic interoperability is to note that "synoptic" describes the envelope into which data elements are placed for transporting them from one place to another, whereas "semantic" describes the content that is placed in the envelope.

Figure 7.1 provides a visual representation comparing the focus of synoptic and semantic interoperability. Both are required to truly share clinical data.

Work on synoptic interoperability such as is contained in HL7v2 has been the most visible and, in many ways, the most

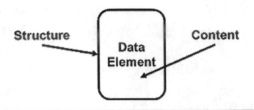

Figure 7.1   **Differences between synoptic and semantic components of data elements.**

successful contribution to the sharing of clinical and administrative health care data. Driven initially by interface design experts and users, the focus of HL7v2 was simply to be able to move data from one system to another. But moving data does not mean that the data collected in one system and moved to another will be able to be used in the second system if the users define the same set of terms differently. The challenge of semantic interoperability is to assure that the definition of the data elements in the first system will be the same when they are used in the second system.

For example, the initial system may capture an observation by a clinician recording in abbreviated notation about the patient as "COLD." If this notation is sent to a second system, a clinician reading the term COLD may have several interpretations:

The patient is COLD, i.e., emotionally distant.
The patient is COLD, i.e., might be shivering during the
    examination.
The patient has a COLD, i.e., exhibits symptoms of an upper
    respiratory infection.
The patient has COLD, i.e., has been diagnosed with
    chronic obstructive lung disease.

Note that it is not only the term "COLD" that is important, but also the context in which it has been used (differing by whether the clinician intended to use "is," "has a," or "has"). So, standards for interoperability must meet two tests: a standard structure for the data element and a standard meaning of that element including the context in which it has been used.

Another example of the importance of context can be found when a physician documents that a patient has "borderline high blood pressure." The list below illustrates the currently more than two dozen ways of describing types of borderline high blood pressure, depending both on meaning of the specific terms used and on the context in which the clinician uses the term. The illustrated terms are all used by clinicians to document the presence of some type of borderline high blood pressure and are captured and stored in patients' medical records.

1. 140/90
2. Accelerated hypertension
3. Arteriolar nephrosclerosis
4. Benign hypertension
5. Benign Intracranial hypertension
6. HBP
7. Borderline high blood pressure
8. Borderline hypertension
9. Chronic hypertension
10. Essential hypertension
11. Elevated BP
12. Familial hypertension
13. Familial primary pulmonary hypertension
14. Genetic hypertension
15. High blood pressure
16. Hypertension – essential
17. Hypertension – malignant
18. Hypertension – renovascular
19. Hypertensive crisis
20. Htn
21. Hyperpiesia, idiopathic hypertension
22. Idiopathic pulmonary hypertension

23. Malignant hypertension
24. Nephrosclerosis – arteriolar
25. PPH; Pregnancy-induced hypertension
26. Primary pulmonary hypertension
27. Primary pulmonary hypertension (PPH)
28. Primary pulmonary vascular disease
29. Pulmonary arterial hypertension, secondary
30. Pulmonary hypertension
31. Renal hypertension
32. Secondary pulmonary hypertension
33. Severe hypertension

A major step toward semantic interoperability begins with establishing standards for coding the data. Chapter 6 described the complexity that was added to clinical documentation with the adoption of ICD-10, a coding scheme intended to introduce more clarity of "meaning" into the data that clinicians use. For the most part, this was accomplished by expanding the descriptive levels of diagnoses (e.g., by adding numeric modifiers to codes). Distinguishing between the "right" hand and the "left" hand, as occurs in ICD-10, for example, is important for diagnostic purposes; fortunately, there is general agreement on what is a "right" hand and what is a "left" hand. For many other even relatively common terms, there is no such universal understanding.

The creation of the Systematized Nomenclature of Medicine (SNOMED-CT) and the Logical Observation Identifiers Names and Codes (LOINC) represent two of the major content standards development efforts that have taken place over the past fifty years. These standards are also called "reference terminologies" and are used in many EMR systems today. In many ways, the development of these standards parallels the development of HL7 as a data structure standard.

The *Systematized Nomenclature of Pathology* (SNOP), first published by the College of American Pathologists (CAP) in

1965, contained terms based on morphology and pathology. In 1975, SNOP was expanded into a more generalized set of terms and became the *Systematized Nomenclature of Medicine* (SNOMED). Over the years more terms were added, and other content coding standards were incorporated to become SNOMED-CT (for Clinical Terms). Like many other branding efforts, however, the standard today is referred to simply as SNOMED-CT, without reference to the terms underlying the initials. As used today, SNOMED-CT:

> Provides a standardized way to represent clinical phrases captured by the clinician and enables automatic interpretation of these. SNOMED CT is a clinically validated, semantically rich, controlled vocabulary that facilitates evolutionary growth in expressivity to meet emerging requirements.[32]
>
> SNOMED-CT currently contains more than 300,000 concepts, 779,000 descriptions, 19 hierarchies, and 1.5 million relationships.[33]

The use of SNOMED-CT became even more embedded into the clinical workflow as a clinical content standard when the federal government mandated its use to meet the requirements for EMR Certification and Meaningful Use Stage 2. SNOMED-CT codes are intended for use by clinicians in their documentation of patient care, and since they are electronic, can also be mapped to ICD-10 codes, which was also mandated.[34]

LOINC, another set of clinical content standards, was initially developed in 1994 by Clem McDonald at the Regenstrief Institute, a nonprofit medical research organization connected with Indiana University. The goal of LOINC was to:

> develop a common terminology for laboratory and clinical observations because there was a growing trend to send clinical data electronically from

laboratories and other data producers to hospitals, physician's offices, and payers who use the data for clinical care and management purposes.[35]

While HL7 focused on the structure of data elements and their transport from one system to another, LOINC (and SNOMED) sought to describe what was "inside" the messages. LOINC was specifically designed to standardize the use of laboratory test codes:

> [T]ests in ... [HL7] messages are identified by means of their internal, idiosyncratic code values. As a result, receiving care system[s] cannot fully "understand" and properly file the results they receive unless they either adopt the producer's test codes (which is impossible if they receive results from multiple sources), or invest in the work to map each result producer's code system to their internal code system.[36]

While SNOMED is a generalized set of standard clinical terms, LOINC focuses on:

> measurements, including laboratory tests, clinical measures like vital signs and anthropometric measures, standardized survey instruments, as well as codes for collections of these items, such as panels, forms, and documents.[37]

> LOINC was identified by the HL7 Standards Development Organization as a preferred code set for laboratory test names in transactions between health care facilities, laboratories, laboratory testing devices, and public health authorities.[38]

While SNOMED and LOINC represent standards for clinical content, there are other content standards that have been developed representing specialized areas of health care. The existence of these additional standards repositories under-scores again the complexity of the health care industry. While financial services industries have two major standards-setting organizations that are working on consolidating standards for financial reporting globally, health care continues with numer-ous organizations setting standards for their own areas.[39] Table 7.1 provides a list of major active standards development areas in the health care industry today.

Recently, the American Medical Association (AMA) in a joint announcement with IBM, initiated the Health Data Model Initiative (HDMI), with three major purposes:

First, it seeks to convene clinical and issue-based com-munities focused on specific problematic areas such as hypertension management and diabetes prevention, aim-ing to develop data best practices for patient-centric care.

Second, there is the development of a clinical validation process, where participants will offer online feedback to help specify data elements and relationships that will then be validated for clinical applicability, according to AMA.

Third, participants will help create a strategy to encode information in the HDMI data model, with reference value sets that can be shared and distributed.[40]

Perhaps this is another indication of the complex challenges facing health care: a multi-organizational effort is being pro-posed essentially on top of all the other efforts already under-way. It is too early to tell the extent to which the HDMI will be able to build on historical standards-creating efforts or how successful it will be in achieving its stated purposes.

The underlying reason for interoperability in health care is the fact that patients are typically seen by many different physicians, in many locations—physicians' offices as well as hospitals—during their lifetimes. Couple this with the observa-tion that high quality clinical care depends not just on what

Table 7.1 Major Areas of Content Standards Activity in Health Care[1]

Standard	Description
HL7v3 Clinical Document Architecture (CDA)	An exchange model for clinical documents such as discharge summaries and progress notes; leverages the use of XML, the HL7 Reference Information Models (RIMs), and coded vocabularies.
National Council for Prescription Drug Programs (NCPDP) Data Dictionary	Data dictionary and data content standards for pharmacy data.
Digital Imaging and Communications in Medicine (DICOM)	A messaging standard for digital images.
Clinical Data Interchange Standards Consortium (CDISC)	An open, multidisciplinary nonprofit organization that has established worldwide industry standards to support the electronic acquisition, exchange, submission and archiving of clinical trials data and metadata for medical and biopharmaceutical product development.
Institute of Electrical and Electronic Engineers (IEEE)	A national organization that develops standards for hospital system interface transactions, including links between critical care bedside instruments and clinical information systems.
Workgroup for Electronic Data Interchange (WEDI)	A subgroup of Accreditation Standards Committee X12 that has been involved in developing electronic data interchange standards for billing transactions.
Current Dental Terminology (CDT)	A coding system developed to report services performed by the dental profession.

(Continued)

Table 7.1 (Continue)   Major Areas of Content Standards Activity in Health Care[1]

Standard	Description
Current Procedural Terminology (CPT)	A comprehensive list of descriptive terms and codes published by the American Medical Association (AMA) and used for reporting diagnostic and therapeutic procedures and other medical services performed by physicians.
International Statistical Classification of Diseases and Related Health Problems, Tenth Revision (ICD-10)	A disease classification system developed and promulgated by the World Health Organization. In the U.S., there are two versions of ICD-10, ICD-10-CM (Clinical Modification) is used for diagnostic coding and contains 68,000 codes, while ICD-10-PCS (Procedure Coding System) is used for coding inpatient procedures and contains 87,000 codes.
North American Nursing Diagnosis Association (NANDA)	A conceptual system that guides the classification of nursing diagnoses.
RxNorm	A clinical drug nomenclature that provides standard names for clinical drugs (active ingredient, strength, and dose form) and for dose forms as administered.
Systematized Nomenclature of Medicine Clinical Terms (SNOMED CT)	A comprehensive clinical terminology and infrastructure that enables a consistent way of capturing, sharing, and aggregating health data across specialties and sites of care.
Logical Observation Identifiers, Names and Codes (LOINC)	A terminology standard for exchanging laboratory and clinical information.

[1] "Data Standards, Data Quality, and Interoperability (2013 update)," Selected excerpts, http://library.ahima.org/doc?oid=107104#.WkUZ_N-nHIU. (Accessed on June 17, 2018.)

happens in a single visit or hospital stay but on what has happened to the patient prior to these events. Clinical data—including documentation of symptoms, diagnoses, and treatments—collected from prior visits or stays should be available at the time of any subsequent visit or stay. This is the foundational rationale for interoperability. But, as the AMA/IBM initiative indicates, we are not there yet.

Notes

1. Abraham Flexner, "Medical Education in the United States and Canada, A Report to the Carnegie Foundation for the Advancement of Teaching Bulletin," Carnegie Foundation, no. 4, 1910. http://archive.carnegiefoundation.org/pdfs/elibrary/Carnegie_Flexner_Report.pdf. (Accessed on June 17, 2018.)
2. See Clement J. McDonald, Paul Tang, and George Hripcsak, "Electronic Health Record Systems," Chapter 12 in Edward Shortliffe and James J. Cimino, eds, *Biomedical Informatics*, 4th ed. London: Springer-Verlag, 2014, p. 393 ff.
3. Margalit Gur-Arie, "A Century of Medical Records (HIT Lessons from History)," *On Health Care Technology*, March 19, 2010. http://onhealthtech.blogspot.com/2010/03/century-of-medical-records.html. (Accessed on June 17, 2018.)
4. Margalit Gur-Arie, "A Century of Medical Records (HIT Lessons from History)," *On Health Care Technology*, March 19, 2010. http://onhealthtech.blogspot.com/2010/03/century-of-medical-records.html. (Accessed on June 17, 2018.)
5. Lawrence L. Weed, "Medical Records That Guide and Teach," *N Engl J Med* 1968; 278:593-600, March 14, 1968. http://www.nejm.org/doi/full/10.1056/NEJM196803142781105. (Accessed on June 17, 2018.)
6. "Dr. Lawrence Weed, Pioneer in Recording Patient Data, Dies at 93," *The New York Times*, June 21, 2017. https://www.nytimes.com/2017/06/21/science/obituary-lawrence-weed-dead-patient-information.html. (Accessed on June 17, 2018.)
7. In the 1960s minicomputers from companies like Digital Equipment Corporation (DEC), Data General, Wang, Apollo and Prime brought computer capabilities to hospital departments

like Pathology, Clinical Laboratories, Pharmacy and Radiology at a price point much less that mainframe systems from companies like IBM. The introduction of personal computers from Apple (1977) and IBM (1981) and their processing capabilities (increasing exponentially to the current day) initiated the demise of mini-computing.

8. "Health IT Dashboard," U.S. Department of Health and Human Services. https://dashboard.healthit.gov/quickstats/quickstats.php. (Accessed on June 17, 2018.)

9. According to one source, in 2016 Epic held ~25% of the market, Cerner had ~25% and Meditech ~17%. Becker Hospital Review. https://www.beckershospitalreview.com/healthcare-information-technology/epic-cerner-hold-50-of-hospital-ehr-market-share-8-things-to-know.html. (Accessed on June 17, 2018.)

10. "The 20 EHR Vendors with the Most Physician Users," *Health Data Management*, September 29, 2017. https://www.health-datamanagement.com/slideshow/the-20-ehr-vendors-with-the-most-physician-users. (Accessed on June 17, 2018.)

11. See Nicholas D. Evans, "The New Scope of Mission-Critical Computing," *CIO*, September 17, 2013. https://www.cio.com/article/2474862/high-performance-computing/the-new-scope-of-mission-critical-computing.html. (Accessed on June 17, 2018.)

12. "How Doctors Feel about Electronic Health Records," A National Physician Poll by Stanford Medicine and The Harris Poll, March 2018. http://med.stanford.edu/content/dam/sm/ehr/documents/EHR-Poll-Presentation.pdf. (Accessed June 12, 2018.)

13. While the failure of any IT application may place an organization at financial risk, few failures risk for human lives. Perhaps the only system comparable to EMRs in which failure may risk human lives would be air traffic control, although even in this case, radar capabilities installed in the plane itself may mitigate some of this risk. When an EMR ceases to function, returning to paper processes can be time consuming and difficult, assuming there are still staff available who even remember how to manage with paper.

14. The challenge of sending data from a source system to a receiving system is not unique to health care. And in fact, early efforts with financial transactions such as sending purchase orders and receiving confirmation that the order had been received, provided a foundation for later work on interoperability standards in health care.

15. "Survey: Patients See 18.7 Different Doctors on Average," Cicison News Wire, article provided by Practice Fusion, April 27, 2010. https://www.prnewswire.com/news-releases/survey-patients-see-187-different-doctors-on-average-92171874.html. (Accessed on June 17, 2018.)

16. "What Is Interoperability?" Definition approved by the Board of the Healthcare Information and Management Systems Society, on April 5, 2013. http://www.himss.org/library/interoperability-standards/what-is. (Accessed on June 17, 2018.)

17. "What Is Interoperability?" Definition approved by the Board of the Healthcare Information and Management Systems Society, on April 5, 2013. http://www.himss.org/library/interoperability-standards/what-is. (Accessed on June 17, 2018.)

18. Gina Kolata, "New Cancer Treatments Lie Hidden Under Mountains of Paperwork," *The New York Times*, May 21, 2018. https://www.nytimes.com/2018/05/21/health/medical-records-cancer.html. (Accessed on June 26, 2018.)

19. Gina Kolata, "New Cancer Treatments Lie Hidden Under Mountains of Paperwork," *The New York Times*, May 21, 2018. https://www.nytimes.com/2018/05/21/health/medical-records-cancer.html. (Accessed on June 26, 2018.)

20. See https://www.ansi.org/about_ansi/introduction/history for a detailed description of the development of the American National Standards Institute (ANSI). (Accessed on June 17, 2018.)

21. The Open Systems Interconnect Model (OSI) is a standards-based reference model that was published in 1984 by both the International Standards Organization and the Telecommunications Standardization Sector of the International Telecommunication Union. The model provides for seven layers of standards for telecommunications and computer systems, ranging from Level 1, the physical layer, up through Layer 7, the applications data layer. For more discussion on the OSI Model, see Keith Shaw, "The OSI Model Explained: How to Understand (and Remember) the 7 Layer Network Model," *Network World*, December 4, 2017. https://www.networkworld.com/article/3239677/lan-wan/the-osi-model-explained-how-to-understand-and-remember-the-7-layer-network-model.html. (Accessed on June 17, 2018.)

22. APL had a close working relationship with MITRE, the company that developed the first "back end" networks to integrate air traffic control systems as part of the SAGE Air Defense system. For more technical details of the UCSF project as well as the commercialization of Simborg and Tolchin's work with a product called StatLan, see http://www.ringholm.com/docs/the_early_history_of_health_level_7_HL7.htm. (Accessed on June 17, 2018.)

23. CJ McDonald, BH Park, L Blevins, "Grocers, Physicians and Electronic Data Processing," *AMA Cont Med Ed Newsl.* 1983; 12:5–8. https://www.lhncbc.nlm.nih.gov/publication/pub9527, McDonald had attempted to publish this editorial several years earlier to no avail. After nine rejections, it was finally published in 1983. (Accessed on June 17, 2018.)

24. René Spronk, "The Early History of Health Level Seven," Ringholm bv, September 5, 2014. http://www.ringholm.com/docs/the_early_history_of_health_level_7_HL7.htm. (Accessed on June 17, 2018.)

25. René Spronk, "The Early History of Health Level Seven," Ringholm bv, September 5, 2014. http://www.ringholm.com/docs/the_early_history_of_health_level_7_HL7.htm. (Accessed on June 17, 2018.)

26. René Spronk, "The Early History of Health Level Seven," Ringholm bv, September 5, 2014. http://www.ringholm.com/docs/the_early_history_of_health_level_7_HL7.htm. (Accessed on June 17, 2018.)

27. Health Level 7 International. http://www.hl7.org/about/index.cfm?ref=common. (Accessed on June 17, 2018.)

28. Corepoint Health, "The HL7 Evolution," 2009, p. 8. https://corepointhealth.com/resource-center/white-papers/evolution-hl7. (Accessed on June 17, 2018.)

29. "What Is HL7 v 3," CDAPro, February 9, 2014. http://www.cdapro.com/know/25096. (Accessed on June 17, 2018.)

30. Corepoint Health, "The HL7 Evolution," 2009, p. 2. https://corepointhealth.com/resource-center/white-papers/evolution-hl7. (Accessed on June 17, 2018.)

31. For a detailed discussion of FHIR see https://www.hl7.org/fhir/summary.html. (Accessed on August 24, 2018.)

32. "What Is SNOMED CT?," SNOMED International https://www.snomed.org/snomed-ct/what-is-snomed-ct. (Accessed on June 17, 2018.)

33. Selena Chavis, "Two Systems, One Direction," *For the Record* 25, no. 14, p. 10, October 2013. http://www.fortherecordmag. com/archives/1013p10.shtml. (Accessed on June 17, 2018.)

34. Amy Helwig, "EHR Certification Criteria for SNOMED CT Will Help Doctors Transition to ICD-10," *HealthIT Buzz*, October 29, 2013. https://www.healthit.gov/buzz-blog/electronic-health-and-medical-records/ehr-certification-criteria-snomed-ct-doctors-transition-icd10/. (Accessed on June 17, 2018.)

35. "Origins of LOINC," The Regenstrief Institute, Inc. https://loinc. org/about/. (Accessed on June 17, 2018.)

36. "Origins of LOINC," The Regenstrief Institute, Inc. https://loinc. org/about/. (Accessed on June 17, 2018.)

37. "Origins of LOINC," The Regenstrief Institute, Inc. https://loinc. org/about/. (Accessed on June 17, 2018.)

38. "FAQ: LOINC and Other Standards," The Regenstrief Institute, Inc. HYPERLINK "https://loinc.org/faq/loinc-and-other-standards/" https://loinc.org/faq/loinc-and-other-standards/. (Accessed on June 17, 2018.)

39. For example, the IASB (International Accounting Standards Board) and FASB (Financial Accounting Standards Board—a U.S.-based standards organization), initiated a convergence project almost 20 years ago, an effort that continues to the present day. See https://www.ifrs.com/overview/general/differences.html (accessed on June 17, 2018) and https://www. accountingtoday.com/news/fasb-continues-engagement-with-iasb-on-ifrs (accessed on June 17, 2018).

40. Mike Milliard, "AMA Initiative Calls for Common Data Model, Uniting Providers, Health IT Firms," Healthcare IT News, October 16, 2017. http://www.healthcareitnews.com/news/ama-initiative-calls-common-data-model-uniting-providers-health-it-firms. (Accessed on June 17, 2018.)

Chapter 8

Privacy and Security

8.1 Introduction

> The health care system cannot deliver effective and
> safe care without deeper digital connectivity. If the
> health care system is connected, but insecure, this
> connectivity could betray patient safety, subjecting
> them to unnecessary risk and forcing them to pay
> unaffordable personal costs.[1]

This opening paragraph from the June 2017 Report of the
Health Care Industry Cybersecurity Task Force lays out one of
the fundamental dilemmas in the health care industry: how to
continue the push toward "deeper digital connectivity" while
at the same time safeguarding health care's computer systems
and the patient data they contain, from ever-increasing cybersecurity threats.

    This chapter explores two different but related complex-
ity issues: (1) the continuing threats of unauthorized access to
patient data; and (2) the unique nature of health care's patient
data that makes it more vulnerable to exposure through data
breaches and inappropriate access than data in many other
industries.

8.2 Threats to Patient Data

There are two types of data that individuals typically wish to keep to themselves: data about their finances and data about their health. While data about an individual's finances can certainly have an impact on status and others' perception of well-being, health care data can have more far-reaching implications. Such data can provide knowledge about an individual's fitness for work, insurability, life style choices, personal history, immunities, and sensitivities, etc. While one's financial data captures a moment in time, one's health data can reflect an entire lifetime.

If an unauthorized person gains access to an individual's financial accounts and illegally transfers funds out of those accounts, the banks or financial institutions hosting the account will typically take responsibility for the loss and restore the amounts taken. So, while the money may be gone for a time and require time and effort to have it restored, there are unlikely to be lasting consequences.

One other area of risk for financial data loss is credit cards, although the value here lies not in the card itself but in the financial data it may contain and the access that comes with knowing the credit card number. Data contained on the card can be replicated and then used without the original card owner's authorization. As with unauthorized financial account access, however, the actual loss of the card data may be short term since most card issuers take some level of responsibility for the loss of the data and any subsequent unauthorized charges made to the card.

Health data, on the other hand, once exposed, cannot be restored. If an individual's HIV status has been revealed, for example, there is simply no way to "undo" the loss—and the consequences of the exposure of health data can extend for years and impact every aspect of an individual's life and often for their entire lifetime. In addition, an individual's health data on file with a provider organization—whether hospital, ancillary provider or physician office—typically contains more than just the individual's health status. A medical record, for example, can contain not only an individual's name, age and address, but identifying data such as social security number, any credit card numbers if a card has been used to pay for services, insurance policy and plan numbers, diagnostic codes, names and addresses of spouses and children, and any other data collected while receiving services from a health care provider. Unauthorized access can enable an intruder to recreate a person's identity from what is stored in their medical record, and subsequently submit false billing claims to both public and private payers or going further, recreate the person's identity and then use it (perhaps in conjunction with credit card data) to collect public benefits, open a bank account, file for income tax refunds, purchase virtually anything available with a credit card, apply for a loan for a car, etc. Unlike bank account or credit card fraud, which can be revealed shortly after the data is exposed through monthly statements or purchases made with the card, it can take months or years before the loss of one's health data becomes apparent.

One measure of the value of health data is to look at how such data is viewed by the "after-market," i.e., those who are interested in purchasing such data after it has been fraudulently exposed. One expert has noted:

> On the dark web, complete medical records typically contain an individual's name, birthdate, social security number, and medical information. These records can sell for as much as (the bitcoin equivalent) of $60 apiece, whereas social security numbers are a mere $15. Stolen credit cards sell for just $1 to $3....[2]

More than 113 million medical records were hacked in 2015 alone, according to data compiled by the Health and Human Services. A newly released report from the Institute for Critical Infrastructure Technology, a cybersecurity think tank, found that some 47% of Americans have had their medical record hacked in the past 12 months.[3]

Data breaches in the health care industry seem to be growing in size and severity. Consider the following:

- Records accessed between 2009 and 2014 averaged about 7 million annually; in 2015, that number jumped to over 94 million, due in part to several particularly large breaches.
- Average cost of data breach per health care record was estimated to be almost $400, twice that of other industries.
- Average annual cost of data breaches in health care from 2009 to 2014 was ~$2 million; in 2015, the cost grew to ~$37 million, again due to several large breaches.
- In the first half of 2017, health care experienced the largest number of breaches (228), followed by financial services (125) and education (118).[4]
- Two particularly large breaches were experienced by Britain's National Health Service[5] and the Anthem Health Insurance Company.[6]
- 91% of health care organizations have suffered at least one data breach in the past two years, 39% have experienced two to five data breaches, and 40% have suffered more than five.[7]

In 2013, another type of "cybersecurity" problem or malware[8] surfaced in the form of ransomware. With typical data breaches, the data is taken or copied from its source and posted elsewhere, intending to be sold on what is essentially a "black market" for data. Once sold, the credit card and social security numbers can be used for purchases or for creating false identities, which themselves can be used to apply for more credit cards, bank loans, etc. Gaining financial rewards from stealing data therefore becomes a multistep process—taking the data, posting or storing it, locating buyers, providing access to the data, and then accepting payment.

Ransomware, on the other hand, works differently. Essentially a hacker takes control of a set of data either by "locking" it (known as locker ransomware) so that the authorized user can't access it or by encrypting it (known as crypto ransomware) so that it can only be accessed using an encryption key. In both cases, the hacker sends a message to the data's owner stating that access to the data will only be re-established after receiving a stipulated payment.[9] Ransomware attacks have increased significantly over the past several years—rising from the 22nd most common form of malware in 2014 to the fifth most common variety in 2017.[10] In 2016, 72% of all malware attacks in health care were ransomware.

It is easy to understand why ransomware is becoming a hacking technology much preferred to stealing personal data. The process of going from "the hack" to "the money" is much more efficient. There is no data to move or even copy; once the data is blocked from access by authorized users and the ransom demand put in place, the hacker simply waits until a payment is processed. Now that bitcoin has become popular as a virtual currency that cannot be easily traced, the anonymity of the person requesting payment is protected.

A recent *Fortune* article provided some insight why health care is such a frequent target both for data breaches and for ransomware demands:

> Health information is simultaneously intensely personal, accompanied by crucial financial information, and universal—after all, health care consumerism isn't so much a choice as it is an ontological necessity of being a human.[11]

In addition to the data itself, there is the challenge of keeping the security infrastructure up to the task of protecting patient data—described by some as a "glacial" process.[12]

> Medicine may be making science fiction-level
> advances; but the systems which house its day-to-day
> information have yet to receive the same 21st cen-
> tury jolt. Protective measures haven't caught up
> with would-be attack methods, and human error—
> whether it be falling for phishing scams or a hospital
> administrator failing to change his or her password—
> continues to be a major hurdle to data security.[13]

One example of the "glacial" progress of health care IT is the continued use of an almost fifty-year-old standard, File Transfer Protocol (FTP).[14] Originally developed in 1971, FTP continues to be used within the health community for transferring files among institutions and individuals. Although there are more recent and secure alternatives available for file transfer, the health care industry's complexity and continuing use of older (and in many cases, unsupported) technologies tends to favor keeping protocols such as FTP in use. The FBI has been so concerned about this problem that in March 2017 it issued a Private Industry Notification with specific warnings about the continued use of FTP.[15]

Another example of health care's glacial change in IT is the continued use of unsupported operating systems for computers attached, for example, to imaging equipment and laboratory devices, although some provider organizations continue to use outdated operating systems for their desktop devices as well. It is not uncommon for health care providers to have Windows NT devices supporting critical patient care equipment even though Microsoft ceased all development work and support for the NT operating systems in 2004. In many cases the rationale for continuing to use NT is "if it still works, then we won't need to replace it," even though more recent versions of Windows provide much more secure environments.

In any industry, leadership and vision at the top of the organization (the so-called "C-Suite") often determines how the organization responds to potential threats to the data that the organization holds either on its own, or in the case of health care, on behalf of its patients. Even though the health care industry is increasingly targeted by cyber criminals, a recent report suggests that there is little leadership or vision in the critical area of cyber security. Consider the following:

- 84% of provider organizations lack a reliable enterprise leader for cybersecurity.
- 11% of provider organizations plan to get a cybersecurity officer in 2018.
- 54% do not conduct regular risk assessments;
- 39% do not carry out regular penetration testing on their firewalls.
- 92% indicated that cybersecurity and the threat of data breach are not major talking points with their board of directors.[16]

With such an extraordinary lack of focus on the security of data assets, including those that provider organizations hold effectively in trust for their patients, it is easy to see why health care organizations are not only such frequent targets for hackers, but are likely to remain so for the foreseeable future.

8.3 Health Insurance Portability and Accountability Act

There is likely no other industry in the American economy for which federal legislation mandates requirements regarding privacy and security so specifically as has happened in health care. When health care began to adopt computerized record keeping for clinical records in the early 1990s, concerns about how to protect patient data became paramount. For example, the report from the National Institute of Medicine, which was cited in Chapter 2, emphasized among other aspects of a computerized patient record, the importance of maintaining the security and privacy of patients' medical records.[17]

The basis for health care data protections lies in the 1996 Health Insurance Portability and Accountability Act (HIPAA).[18] This legislation was intended as a broad-based effort to reform protections for the collection and management of patient data.

Two broad objectives were included in HIPAA:

1. Title I – Ensure that individuals would be able to maintain their health insurance between jobs (referred to as health care *portability*).
2. Title II – Ensure the security and confidentiality of patient information/data, and in addition mandate uniform standards for electronic data transmission of administrative and financial data relating to patient health information (this is the *accountability* portion of the legislation).[19]

Regulations released by the federal government to guide the implementation of the HIPAA legislation are grouped into three areas:

Administrative simplification: requires the creation of uniform standards and requirements for the electronic transmission of health information

Security: requires providers and others who maintain health information to maintain the security and integrity of individually identifiable health information

Privacy: sets forth general rules for the uses and disclosures of individually identifiable health information by providers and others[20]

The complexity of the health care industry is certainly increased by the security and privacy provisions contained in HIPAA. The impact on every player in health care has been significant, and anyone interested or involved in the health care industry not only needs to be aware of HIPAA requirements, but be prepared to accommodate HIPAA requirements in whatever products or services they provide.

It is no coincidence that the enactment of HIPAA occurred in about the same timeframe as the initial efforts were underway to computerize patient records. When patient health information was collected, stored and managed on paper, one had to physically retrieve the paper record from the medical records department in order to read it. Given the volume of paper generated by patients with long histories of disease and/or care, one might argue there was a reasonable amount of security and confidentiality associated with paper records. With computerization, however, this type of physical security no longer exists, and the "accountability" aspects of HIPAA became very important.

Here is a "bottom line" summary of the rights HIPAA has provided to patients:

- Health care providers and insurance companies must explain how they'll use and disclose health information.
- Patients can ask for copies of all their health information, make appropriate changes, and ask for a history of any unusual disclosures.
- Patients must give formal consent for any sharing of their health information.
- Patients have the right to complain to the Department of Health and Human Services (HHS) about HIPAA rules' violations.
- Health information is to be used only for health purposes.
- When health information gets shared, only the minimum necessary amount of information should be disclosed.
- Psychotherapy records get an extra level of protection.[21]

Two concepts form the core of HIPAA regulations, Protected Health Information (PHI) and Covered Entities and their Business Associates:

Protected Health Information (PHI) includes any individually identifiable health information transmitted or maintained in any form or medium by a Covered Entity or its Business Associate; a subset of PHI is labeled as individually identifiable health information which includes any information related to an individual's physical or mental health or the provision of or payment for health care, and identifies the individual.[22]

Covered Entity includes health care providers, health care plans (including insurance companies and HMOs) and clearing houses which process health data according to electronic standards. In addition, covered entities in the process of managing their business may engage Business Associates to assist with health care activities and functions, and these entities must have a written contract, or other arrangement, that establishes specifically what the Business Associate has been engaged to do and requires the Business Associate to comply with the regulation's requirements to protect the privacy and security of protected health information. In addition to these contractual obligations, Business Associates are directly liable for compliance with certain provisions of the HIPAA Rules.[23]

As one might imagine, there is a wealth of materials available on HIPAA legislation and the resulting implementation rules. While too extensive to review in more detail here, it should be noted that the consequences for not complying with the rules can be significant. The American Recovery and Reinvestment Act of 2009 (ARRA) established a civil penalty structure for HIPAA violations according to specific tiered levels[24] (see Table 8.1).

Complaints about HIPAA violations are typically made to the Office of Civil Rights (OCR) in the U.S. Department of Health and Human Services (HHS) and can come from

Table 8.1 Penalties for HIPAA Violations

HIPAA Violation	Minimum Penalty	Maximum Penalty
Individual did not know (and by exercising reasonable diligence would not have known) they violated HIPAA	$100 per violation, with an annual maximum of $25,000 for repeat violations (Note: maximum that can be imposed by State Attorneys General regardless of the type of violation)	$50,000 per violation, with an annual maximum of $1.5M
HIPAA violation due to reasonable cause and not due to willful neglect	$1,000 per violation, with an annual maximum of $100,000 for repeat violations	$50,000 per violation, with an annual maximum of $1.5M
HIPAA violation due to willful neglect but violation is corrected within the required time period	$10,000 per violation, with an annual maximum of $250,000 for repeat violations	$50,000 per violation, with an annual maximum of $1.5M
HIPAA violation is due to willful neglect and is not corrected	$50,000 per violation, with an annual maximum of $1.5M	$50,000 per violation, with an annual maximum of $1.5M

individuals or groups of patients or from public media exposure. The subsequent investigation can focus on any or all of the following areas:

- Administrative security
- Physical security
- Technical security
- Structural requirements
- Policies, procedures, and documentation requirements[25]

Privacy issues and security issues, while regulated under the same set of legislations, present two different challenges:

1. **Privacy** – the HIPAA Privacy rule covers protected health information regardless of where it is stored:

   > The Privacy rule protects all "individually iden-tifiable health information" held or transmitted by a covered entity or its business associate, in any form or media, whether electronic, paper, or oral. The Privacy rule calls this information "protected health information (PHI)."[26]

   An excellent discussion of the Privacy rule can be found in the HHS 18-page *Summary of the HIPAA Privacy Rule*.[27]

2. **Security** – the HIPAA Security rule covers electronic protected health information, so information transmit-ted orally or on paper is not covered. The Security rule is more involved than the Privacy rule since it requires covered entities to establish policies and procedures to ensure that protected health information is only available to authorized users and steps are taken by the organiza-tion not only to track who is viewing this electronic infor-mation but to prevent unauthorized persons from having access. Here is a summary of what covered entities are expected to do to comply with the Security rule:

   - Ensure the confidentiality, integrity, and availability of all ePHI they create, receive, maintain, or transmit.
   - Identify and protect against reasonably anticipated threats to the security or integrity of the information.
   - Protect against reasonably anticipated, impermissible uses or disclosures.
   - Ensure compliance by their workforce.[28]

The results of HIPAA enforcement actions from April 2003 to January 2018, as reported by the Department of Health and Human Services include:

■ 173,426 HIPAA complaints received.
■ 871 compliance reviews completed.
■ 97% (168,780) of these cases resolved.
■ In over 25,695 cases, changes were required in privacy practices and corrective actions by, or providing technical assistance to, HIPAA covered entities and their business associates.
■ Settled or imposed a civil money penalty in 53 cases resulting in a total dollar amount of $75,229,182.00.
■ Investigated complaints against many different types of entities including: national pharmacy chains, major medical centers, group health plans, hospital chains, and small provider offices.[29]

HIPAA reports cover both security and privacy violations. Data breaches, on the other hand, cover hacking and ransomware demands as well. Over the past 2–3 years the number of records breached appears to be stabilizing, although the actual number of breaches continues to increase:

2016 was a particularly bad year for health care data breaches. The largest health care data breaches of 2016 were nowhere near the scale of those seen in 2015—16,471,765 records were exposed compared to 113,267,174 records in 2015—but more covered entities reported breaches than in any other year since [the Office of Civil Rights] started publishing breach summaries on its "Wall of Shame" in 2009. 2016 ranks as the second worst year in terms of the number of patient and health plan members' records that have been exposed in a single year.[30]

Breach reporting increased slightly between 2016 and 2017, although the number of records compromised was significantly less—the result of fewer very large breaches. Data breaches in both 2016 and 2017 averaged more than one per day. On average, it took 308 days for an organization to discover it had suffered a breach in 2017. In one incident, a hospital employee was inappropriately accessing patient records for 14 years before being discovered.[31]

An *Indiana Business Journal* report on data security in health care was sparked in part by several significant data breaches for Indiana companies.[32] Using estimates developed by the American Action Forum, the report estimated that the overall cost of health care data breaches since 2009 likely ranged from $17 billion to over $37 billion, which covers the $19 billion allocated by the federal government in incentives to health care providers to adopt electronic medical records. This estimate likely does not include the additional costs health care providers are incurring every day from the purchase of new security products and services and the staffing needed to oversee security measures which are now routine at health care providers all over the country.

A study released in early 2017 provided additional data on the challenges of data breaches:

- 26% of U.S. consumers have had their personal medical information stolen.
- 50% of breach victims had their identities stolen and paid on average approximately $2,500 in out-of-pocket costs per incident.
- 36% of breaches occurred in hospitals; over 20% occurred in other settings, including urgent-care clinics, pharmacies, physician's offices, and health insurers.
- 50% of consumers found out about their data breaches on their own; 33% were alerted by the organization in which it occurred, but only 15% were alerted by a government agency.[33]

Losses resulting from credit card theft are usually covered under identity theft provisions above the first $50 by the organization issuing the card. Unfortunately, medical identity theft typically does not have similar coverage.

Privacy and security mandates are likely much more stringent in health care than in any other industry. There is nothing more personal than an individual's health information. With HIPAA legislation and subsequent HHS rules, it is clear that everyone involved in the health care industry must meet the standards the federal government has established, or risk serious consequences.

It is ironic that the advent of IT investments in health care, particularly with the implementation of EMR systems, has brought an extraordinary set of privacy and security measures mandated by the federal government. Unfortunately, these measures have not prevented health care from becoming one of the most frequent targets of unauthorized access to personal data.

This is truly a "double-edged" sword for electronic medical records—facilitating access by authorized persons such as physicians, who need that access to provide high quality care, while at the same time risking the exposure of that data to ever-changing forms of unauthorized access through data breaches and (as the case with ransomware) even blackmail.

Notes

1. Health Care Industry Cybersecurity Task Force, "Report on Improving Cybersecurity in the Health Care Industry," June 2017. https://www.phe.gov/Preparedness/planning/CyberTF/Documents/report2017.pdf. (Accessed on June 17, 2018.) In 2015, Congress passed the Cybersecurity Act of 2015, which created the Health Care Industry Cybersecurity (HCIC) Task Force.
2. Christina Farr, "On the Dark Web, Medical Records Are a Hot Commodity," *FastCompany*, July 7, 2016. https://www.fastcompany.com/3061543/on-the-dark-web-medical-records-are-a-hot-commodity. (Accessed on June 17, 2018.)

3. Christina Farr, "On the Dark Web, Medical Records Are a Hot Commodity," *FastCompany*, July 7, 2016. https://www.fastcompany.com/3061543/on-the-dark-web-medical-records-are-a-hot-commodity. (Accessed on June 17, 2018.)

4. For more details, see Julie Spitzer, "918 Cyberattacks So Far This year: 6 Things to Know," Health IT and CIO Report, Beckers Hospital Review, September 20, 2017. http://www.beckershospitalreview.com/cybersecurity/918-cyberattacks-so-far-this-year-6-things-to-know.html. (Accessed on June 17, 2018.)

5. A reported 26 million records were exposed in the NHS breach. See *The Telegraph*, March, 17, 2017. https://www.telegraph.co.uk/news/2017/03/17/security-breach-fears-26-million-nhs-patients/. (Accessed on June 17, 2018.)

6. A reported 79 million records were exposed in the Anthem Health breach. See Threatpost. https://threatpost.com/anthem-agrees-to-settle-2015-data-breach-for-115-million/126527/. (Accessed on June 17, 2018.)

7. Cited in Jeff Goldman, "91 Percent of Healthcare Organizations Suffered Data Breaches in the Past Two Years," eSecurity Planet, May 12, 2015. http://www.esecurityplanet.com/network-security/91-percent-of-healthcare-organizations-suffered-data-breaches-in-the-past-two-years.html. (Accessed on June 17, 2018.)

8. Ransomware is a specific form of "malware," which is a short-hand form of "malicious software," and refers to any harmful or intrusive software, including computer viruses, worms, Trojan horses, ransomware, spyware, adware, scareware, etc. For more discussion, see Josh Fruhlinger, "What Is Ransomware? How It Works and How to Remove It," CSOonline, November 13, 2017. https://www.csoonline.com/article/3236183/ransomware/what-is-ransomware-how-it-works-and-how-to-remove-it.html. (Accessed on June 17, 2018.)

9. Kevin Savage, Peter Coogan and Hon Lau, "The Evolution of Ransomware," Symantec, Version 1.0 – August 6, 2015, p. 5. http://www.symantec.com/content/en/us/enterprise/media/security_response/whitepapers/the-evolution-of-ransomware.pdf. (Accessed on June 17, 2018.)

10. 2017 Data Breach Investigations Report, 10th ed. Verizon. https://www.verizondigitalmedia.com/blog/2017/07/2017-verizon-data-breach-investigations-report/. (Accessed on June 17, 2018.)

11. Sy Mukherjee, "Why Health Care Is Especially Vulnerable to Ransomware Attacks," Fortune.com, May 15, 2017. http://fortune.com/2017/05/15/ransomware-attack-healthcare/. (Accessed on June 17, 2018.)

12. Sy Mukherjee, "Why Health Care Is Especially Vulnerable to Ransomware Attacks," Fortune.com, May 15, 2017. http://fortune.com/2017/05/15/ransomware-attack-healthcare/. (Accessed on June 17, 2018.)

13. Sy Mukherjee, "Why Health Care Is Especially Vulnerable to Ransomware Attacks," Fortune.com, May 15, 2017. http://fortune.com/2017/05/15/ransomware-attack-healthcare/. (Accessed on June 17, 2018.)

14. For a more in-depth discussion of FTP, see Pamela Statz, "FTP for Beginners," *Wired*, February 15, 2010. https://www.wired.com/2010/02/ftp_for_beginners/. (Accessed on June 17, 2018.)

15. "Cyber Criminals Targeting FTP Servers to Compromised Protected Health Information," Federal Bureau of Investigation, March 22, 2017, PIN Number 170322-001. https://info.publicintelligence.net/FBI-PHI-FTP.pdf. (Accessed on June 17, 2018.)

16. Bill Siwicki, "Black Book: 84% of Hospitals Lack a Dedicated Security Leader," Healthcare IT News, December 18, 2017. http://www.healthcareitnews.com/news/black-book-84-hospitals-lack-dedicated-security-leader. (Accessed on June 17, 2018.)

17. Richard S. Dick, Elaine B. Steen, and Don E. Detmer, eds., *The Computer-Based Patient Record*. Washington, DC: Institute of Medicine, National Academy Press, 1997.

18. 45 CFR § 160.103 Definitions (2013 HIPAA Omnibus Rule).

19. For more in-depth discussion, see "HIPAA Background," University of Chicago Medical Center. http://hipaa.bsd.uchicago.edu/background.html. (Accessed on June 17, 2018.)

20. "Health Insurance Portability and Accountability Act (HIPAA)," New York State Office of Mental Health. http://www.omh.ny.gov/omhweb/hipaa/. (Accessed on June 17, 2018.)

21. Daniel J. DeNoon, "HIPAA Rules Explained," WebMD, April 22, 2003. http://www.webmd.com/healthy-aging/news/20030422/hipaa-rules-explained. (Accessed on June 17, 2018.)

22. "Protected Health Information," U.S. Department of Health and Human Services. https://www.hhs.gov/hipaa/for-professionals/privacy/special-topics/de-identification/index.html#protected. (Accessed on June 17, 2018.)

23. "Covered Entities and Business Associates," U.S. Department of Health and Human Services. http://www.hhs.gov/ocr/privacy/hipaa/understanding/coveredentities/. (Accessed on June 17, 2018.)

24. "HIPAA Administrative Simplification," Regulation Text, 45 CFR Parts 160, 162, and 164. (Unofficial Version, as amended through March 26, 2013.) Section 160.404. U.S. Department of Health and Human Services. https://www.hhs.gov/sites/default/files/hipaa-simplification-201303.pdf. (Accessed on June 17, 2018.)

25. "HIPAA Violation Equals Trouble for Healthcare Organizations," Iron Mountain, Inc. http://www.ironmountain.com/Knowledge-Center/Reference-Library/View-by-Document-Type/General-Articles/H/HIPAA-Violation-Equals-Trouble-for-Healthcare-Organizations.aspx#sthash.UpAlVLxw.dpuf. (Accessed on June 17, 2018.)

26. 45 CFR § 160.103 Definitions (2013 HIPAA Omnibus Rule).

27. "Summary of the HIPAA Privacy Rule," U.S. Department of Health and Human Services. https://www.hhs.gov/hipaa/for-professionals/privacy/laws-regulations/index.html. (Accessed on June 17, 2018.)

28. 45 C.F.R. § 164.306(a) Security standards: General rules.

29. "Enforcement Highlights," U.S. Department of Health and Human Services. https://www.hhs.gov/hipaa/for-professionals/compliance-enforcement/data/enforcement-highlights/index.html. (Accessed on June 17, 2018.)

30. "Largest Healthcare Data Breaches of 2016," *HIPAA Journal,* January 4, 2017. https://www.hipaajournal.com/largest-health-care-data-breaches-of-2016-8631/. (Accessed on June 17, 2018.)

31. "5.6M Patient Records Breached in 2017 as Healthcare Struggles to Proactively Protect Health Data," Proteneus, January 23, 2018. https://www.protenus.com/press/press-release/56m-patient-records-breached-in-2017-as-healthcare-struggles-to-pro-actively-protect-health-data. (Accessed on June 28, 2018.)

32. J.K. Wall, "Costs of Data Breaches, Just This Year, Outstrip Subsidies to Digitize Health Care," *Indianapolis Business Journal,* August 7, 2015. http://www.ibj.com/blogs/12-the-dose/post/54343-costs-of-data-breaches-just-this-year-outstrip-subsidies-to-digitize-health-care. (Accessed on June 17, 2018.) Major data breaches in the state of Indiana included unauthorized access to 80,000,000 records in Anthem Blue Cross, a

three-time breach affecting 68,000 records from St. Vincent's Health, 43,000 records lost from a laptop belonging to Aspire Indiana, 38,000 records from stolen hard drives from the Indiana State Medical Society, and 3.9 million records from Medical Informatics Engineering.

33. For more details about health care data breaches and their impact on individuals, see "One in Four U.S. Consumers Have Had Their Healthcare Data Breached, Accenture Survey Reveals," Accenture LLP, February 20, 2017. https://newsroom. accenture.com/news/one-in-four-us-consumers-have-had-their-healthcare-data-breached-accenture-survey-reveals.htm. (Accessed on June 17, 2018.)

Chapter 9

Politics Large and Small

9.1 Introduction

Politics in its derivation from the original Greek is about governance, which in turn is based on the ability for some individuals to exert control over others. Put another way, politics is essentially about power relationships.[1] Power relationships among individuals in an organizational setting stem from a perceived hierarchy of rights and privileges (often reinforced by differences in compensation); if that hierarchy persists, some will think themselves able to decide the priority of tasks to be done as well as the processes needed to complete them and expect others to follow their lead.

This chapter considers two types of politics: (1) politics that occur primarily at the national level through relationships among members of Congress, the Executive and the Judicial branches of government;[2] and (2) politics that occur within organizational settings—and most specifically the hospital and health system organizations that provide health care services (also known as "provider organizations"). Limiting the discussion to these two areas is appropriate since there are two primary political components that influence health care complexity: (1) the actions of the Congress, the Executive and the

Judicial branches of government through policies and funding they enact, determines to a great extent how health care services are provided in this country and who pays for them; and (2) the behavior of individual provider organizations determines how health care services are delivered to individual patients.

9.2 National Political Influences

Health care expenditures in the United States in 2016 exceeded \$3.3 trillion, or almost 18% of the United States' total Gross Domestic Product.[3] As documented in the Center for Medicare and Medicaid Services' National Healthcare Expenditures Report:

> The largest shares of total health spending were sponsored by the federal government (28.3%) and the households (28.1%). The private business share accounted for 19.9% of total health care spending, state and local governments accounted for 16.9%, and other private revenues accounted for 6.7%.[4]

Clearly, federal government policies and practices as proposed and approved by the Congress, implemented by the Executive Branch and reviewed by the Judicial Branch, have a major impact on what happens in the health care industry.

The history of the federal government's involvement in the health care industry is extensive, with Medicare and Medicaid legislation in the 1965 being primary milestones. Between World War II and the Medicare and Medicaid legislation, health care insurance was provided primarily through the workplace, with sporadic efforts at the state and local levels for those receiving cash assistance.[5]

In 2010, Congress passed PL 111-148, known as the Patient Protection and Affordable Care Act (ACA) which introduced the concept of the health care insurance marketplace and provided for a substantial expansion in the Medicaid program.[6] The ACA contained new regulations for all health plans which prevented insurance companies from denying coverage to people for any reason, including health status, and from charging higher premiums based on health status and gender; in addition the ACA required that most individuals have health insurance beginning in 2014, and stipulated penalties for employers that did not offer affordable coverage to their employees, with exceptions for small employers.[7] Health care insurance premium support and cost-sharing subsidies for poverty-level recipients were also an important component of the ACA.

On the other side of the equation, several taxes were imposed to cover portions of the ACA's costs. These included taxes on insurance companies, pharmaceutical manufacturers, and medical device manufacturers. In addition, taxes were imposed on high income individuals and on employers offering generous and focused health benefits that were limited to high income employees (labeled as the "Cadillac tax").

What is important about the ACA is that its passage by Democrats without a single Republican vote displayed the power of the political party in control of the Congress (the Democrats) at the time. After gaining control of the House in 2011, the Republicans tried repeatedly to repeal the ACA (by then labeled as "Obamacare"), stymied initially by Democratic control of the Senate (until 2015) and then by President Obama until he left office at the end of 2016.[8] When Donald Trump became President in 2017, House Republicans again mounted an effort to repeal the ACA (or at least to repeal major parts of it), succeeding with a close approval vote in May 2017 (with 217 in favor and 213 opposed) in the House, but failing by single vote in the Senate.[9]

When the efforts to repeal the ACA in its entirety have fallen short, the Republican strategy shifted to a focus on changing specific components of the program. To date these have included:

1. Elimination of the individual mandate which required everyone (including healthy individuals) to purchase health care insurance.
2. Cut the marketing budget for the ACA programs by 90% and substantially reducing the time period for re-enrollment.
3. Through executive action, permited insurance companies to offer "junk" health insurance with high deductibles and limited coverage.
4. Permitted states to enact work requirements in order for recipients to receive health insurance coverage.
5. Permitted states to require recipients to re-register each year in order to receive health insurance benefits.[10]

These efforts to target the repeal of specific portions of the ACA have clearly had an impact. Premiums have increased—significantly in some states—as healthy individuals are no longer required to purchase health insurance and overall the number of those uninsured has increased as well.[11]

Why does all this matter in a discussion about the complexity of the health care industry? First, consider the fact that the ACA as passed by both houses of Congress and signed by then President Obama ran to about 2,700 pages, and the subsequent rules required in order to interpret and implement the bill added another ~20,000 pages (although there is lots of opportunity to add and subtract pages of rules depending on whether you count proposed versus implemented, etc.).[12] Regardless of the minutiae of counting pages, the ACA as implemented (including legislation and rules) was a highly complex set of documents. As one online commenter noted, "Any law designed to control a system that affects all Americans is bound to require quite a bit of thought and accompanying documentation."[13]

The politics around the ACA were intense at the time and have become even more so with the transition to a new Administration in 2017. As noted above, the initial ACA legislation passed without a single Republican vote; in subsequent years, the House of Representatives has made more than 70 attempts to repeal the ACA, the Supreme Court debated it on 4 occasions, and the controversy over the ACA was at the center of a 2-week federal government shutdown in 2013.

Republican opposition to Obamacare and their numerous attempts at repeal was (and continues to be) based on ideological, economic and historical factors.[14]

Ideological – One of the fundamental principles of Obamacare was that of "redistributive economics,": some participants will need to incur higher insurance premium costs in part to cover the subsidies that the government provided for lower income individuals who purchased coverage through government-run marketplaces. This approach presented a fundamental challenge to Republicans who in general champion smaller government and typically object to the taxation of higher income individuals in order to specifically support lower income earners.

Economic – Much of the debate about Obamacare has focused on economics: in essence, who "wins" and who "loses." The percentage of uninsured Americans declined from 16% in 2010 to 11% in 2016, so many of those previously uninsured were able to get coverage. On the other hand, premiums for health care coverage were predicted to increase by over 20% or more in some situations. Insurers claimed they were incurring losses since more older and sicker persons and fewer healthy persons signed up than were anticipated. Those healthy persons who did sign up were facing higher premiums due to the larger than expected number of persons needing care. Republicans saw this as a never-ending upward spiral— ever higher premiums discouraged healthy individuals from purchasing policies, insurance companies continued to raise rates, further discouraging healthy participants, government subsidies would have to increase in order to keep insurance companies from exiting the markets, and so on, until the system simply collapsed.

Historical – Opposition to government-sponsored health insurance has been evident since the end of World War II. President Truman's proposal for an "expansion of our existing compulsory social insurance system" to cover essentially all Americans, met with strong resistance, particularly from The American Medical Association. Such proposals were labeled as "socialized medicine," associated with communists in an era in which anti-communism and anti-communist rhetoric was prevalent. Even with the passage of major legislative initiatives such as Medicaid and Medicare in the 1960s, opposition to so-called "entitlement" programs has continued. Republican House Speaker Paul Ryan's position in December 2017 was that "the ultimate aim of Republican lawmakers—and their number one priority in January—is to shrink the Medicare program that provides health insurance to the elderly and disabled."[15]

The labels of "redistributive economics" and "socialized medicine" seem to be at the heart of conservative resistance not only to the ACA, but to virtually any formal role for government in the provision of health care to its citizens, preferring at the extreme to leave decisions about who pays for health care and how much to "market-driven" processes. Conservatives' steadfast adherence to these positions and liberal's equally steadfast opposition often overshadow any attempt to discuss provisions of health care services that would require compromises to be successful in the longer run. All of this adds complexity to the health care industry.

The other major piece of national legislation that has impacted the health care industry was the American Recovery and Reinvestment Act (ARRA) of 2009, which was enacted to stimulate the American economy in the wake of the significant economic downturn that occurred in 2008. As part of the passage of the ARRA, the health care industry received an expanded investment in health care generally, with the provision for a ~$30 billion investment in health care information technology—also known as The Health Information Technology for Economic and Clinical Health (HITECH) Act.[16]

The HITECH legislation provided specific incentives designed to stimulate the adoption of electronic health record (EHR)[17] systems by health care providers, and by anticipating the increased exchange of patient information broadened the privacy and security provisions and non-compliance enforcement provisions that had been previously enacted through the 1996 Health Insurance Portability and Accountability Act (HIPAA).

There are likely two major reasons why the ACA and the earlier HITECH legislation significantly enhanced the complexity of the health care industry:

1. Health care affects everyone, and as a result everyone has an opinion about how health care services should be provided, by whom, where, and who should pay for them. Bringing such diversity into a comprehensive program is a significant challenge, and one that few other industries face.

2. Since World War II, our country has had a history of third-party payments for health care services (over 70% of health care expenditures in 2015 were made by third parties such as the federal, state and local governments and private businesses[18]) and, as was noted earlier, the amount of money spent on health care is massive. But in fact, "third-party" payments are in the end paid for by tax payers, both through taxation and through consumer prices that are in part impacted by how much private businesses spend on the health care of their employees.

So not only is everyone impacted by health care (their own as well as often that of their families and friends), but the massive cost of providing health care services impacts everyone as well. As a result, the politics involved in providing payments for health care services are both intense and complex and are impacted in ways not found in other industries.

9.3 Organizational Politics

The organizations that deliver health care services (typically labeled "provider organizations") have their own political challenges (i.e., internal power relationships) which contribute directly to the complexity of the industry. These can be traced to a fundamental hierarchical conflict that is typically not found in other industries: the overlapping, complementary and often conflicting roles that are held by managers and by clinicians.

Chapter 3 discussed the unique role that physicians (and by extension, other clinical professionals) play within health care provider organizations. The actual delivery of a health care service takes place during the relationship that is established between the clinician and the patient. The relationships among physicians, nurses, and other clinical professionals (e.g., pharmacists, respiratory therapists, social workers) and even among clinical specialties (e.g., surgeons, internists, oncologists, etc.) are complex in themselves. While physicians who admit patients to hospitals are typically the "top of the heap," other professionals and specialists (including nurses and pharmacists) are often called on to serve as a "check and balance" on, or extensions to, decisions that physicians make.[19]

There are examples of industries that have both professional roles and management roles, although for the most part it is typically quite clear that one set of roles has predominant oversight responsibilities *vis-à-vis* the other. For example, in professional organizations such as large legal firms, lawyers deliver services and a small cadre of managers "manage the office." In this example, the professionals, (some as partners/owners) have clear and unfettered oversight on all the firms'

operations. At the other end of the scale are educational institutions (including both universities and K-12 systems) in which
professionals (i.e., the teachers) deliver services (i.e., teaching)
while the managers (e.g., a university president or superinten-
dent of schools) have clear oversight responsibilities that tend
to focus on the administrative details of actually running the
organization on a day-to-day basis. Although it is important to
note that "hire/fire" decisions can become highly political as
decisions about who is "qualified" and who is "needed" add a
level of political complexity.

The situation is unique with clinicians in the health care
industry. Clinically trained professionals (which include not
only physicians but nurses, pharmacists, respiratory therapists, and social workers) deliver the service to the client,
often in 1:1 situations. Although some clinicians (e.g., physical
therapists, social workers, and nurses on occasion) operate
independently through their own corporate structures, many
professionals, including physicians, are increasingly employed
by provider organizations.[20]

Financial incentives and the ability to deliver quality services are typically well aligned in many professional organizations, but historically less so in health care provider
organizations. In those situations where the physicians, for
example, are not employed by the provider organization, the
financial management and service delivery objectives can be
in direct competition.

Historically, physicians have operated their practices independent of the hospitals and health systems to which they
admit their patients, although as discussed in Chapter 3, that
has changed significantly in recent years. Within physicians'
own practice environments, compensation has historically
come from each office visit and each procedure they performed—often labeled as "fee-for-service" payments. As such,
there has been a financial incentive to perform as many visits
and procedures as possible—the more "services" performed,
the greater the "fees" received.

This approach has been widely credited with increasing the overall cost of health care delivered in the United States. In fact, some argue that the "fee-for-service" payment model has generated

> [I]nadequate, unnecessary, uncoordinated, and inefficient care and suboptimal business processes [that] eat up at least 35%—and maybe over 50%—of the more than $3 trillion that the country spends annually on health care. That suggests more than $1 trillion is being squandered.[21]

While this is a harsh statement, the fact is that when anyone is paid "by the task," you can be confident that to the extent possible, more tasks will be performed, sometimes whether they are needed or not.

In recent years, as noted in Chapter 3, physicians' relationships to the hospitals and health systems to which they refer and admit their patients have changed significantly. As of July 2016, 42% of all practicing physicians in the United States were employed by hospitals and health systems—a significant increase over the prior 3-year period accompanied by a significant decrease in physician ownership of practices. Part of this change is due to the frenzied physician practice acquisition process by hospitals and health systems in recent years. Between July 2012 and July 2016, for example, 36,000 practices were acquired by hospitals and health systems, a 100% increase over a four year period. Almost 30% of all physician practices are now owned by hospitals and health systems.[22]

A primary motivation behind hospitals' and health systems' acquisition of physician practices is the ability to increase their control over the supply of patients—the patient admitting and referral processes—and thereby adding to their control over physicians and provide a way to improve their management of financial risk. In addition, the ACA legislation provided for the formation of Accountable Care Organizations

(ACOs)—groupings of hospitals and physician practices that are designed to establish accountability for the quality of care, incentivized by Medicare payment arrangements designed to encourage coordination of care between hospitals, home care, skilled nursing facilities and physician practices.[23]

A second motivation has been revenue enhancement for hospital-based services. A recent study found that Medicare reimbursement for three specific health care services, cardio-vascular imaging, colonoscopy, and evaluation and management (E&M) services[24] is consistently higher when performed in a hospital-based department versus a physician's office—in many cases even when risk adjusted for hospital-based care.[25] So a strategy of acquiring a physician practice and relabeling it as a hospital department can bring immediate financial benefits to the hospital.

A third motivation for hospitals to acquire physician practices is the fact that the financial risk for providing care has been consistently shifting from the payers (who bore the risk under fee-for-service arrangements) to the providers. This can be seen in federal government payment strategies starting with the implementation of Diagnosis-Related Groups (DRGs) by the Health Care Financing Administration in the early 1980s.[26] The DRGs represent one of the early attempts by the federal government to shift payments for health care from strictly "fee-for-service" to a model in which the financial risk is increasingly borne by the provider organizations.[27] More recent federal initiatives such as "value-based care" and "bundled payments" have continued the shift of financial risk from the payers to the providers.[28] (This initiative is discussed in more detail in Chapter 10.)

If hospitals and health systems are to be sustainable organizations while bearing increasing risks for the costs of care, they must be able to control more of the care process. Hence, acquiring physician practices and other strategies such as establishing their own captive insurance companies and incorporating home care companies and sub-acute care facilities within their organizational portfolios, is a sensible business strategy, while at the same increasing substantially the complexity of their operations.

All health care is ultimately personal. Concerns about one's own (and one's family's) health care, and who will pay for needed care, make health care both intense and complex. In no other industry do we see this combination of factors influencing both national level policies and organizational level decision-making. The passage of the ACA in 2009 by a Democratic-controlled Congress, the subsequent numerous attempts by Republicans to repeal it, the legislation passed in April 2017 by a Republican-controlled Congress (the American Health Care Act) and the continuing efforts to reduce the federal government's cost of providing health care demonstrate both the attention and the complexity of dealing with health care financing.

At the organizational level, the trend toward more physicians being employed by hospitals and health systems is likely to continue. Politics at this level generally focuses on "who is in charge," the managers or the clinicians. Historically, the physician's judgment about how to care for his/her patients has been paramount (consistent with their role as Knowledge Workers discussed in Chapter 3), with little regard for cost (except for the tendency of fee-for-service reimbursement to increase visits and procedures and therefore physician incomes). That independence may be challenged by hospital and health system managers concerned about the "bottom line" of their organizations. No one argues that high quality health services need to be maintained, but managers must balance that goal with overseeing and sustaining an enterprise that needs to have a positive "bottom line." While one would expect that managers and their employed physicians would be more likely to be on the same page, physicians are not likely to give up their historical commitment to what's right for their patients even if there is an adverse impact on the cost of care. The complexity of the manager/physician relationship doesn't go away simply because the physician now works for the manager.

Regardless of employment arrangements, managers will continue to be rewarded for the most part by achieving a positive financial "bottom line," and clinicians will continue to be rewarded (in financial terms, especially if they are employed by a hospital or health system, but additionally in terms of their own gratification and their reputation with their peers) for the most part by achieving successful patient outcomes.

9.4 Power Shifts in How Organizations Make Decisions about IT Investments

Historically, decisions about IT investments in the health care industry, particularly in provider organizations, have been made by the IT professionals and the executive management. This process worked well when the decisions were being made about admissions systems, or patient billing systems, or financial management systems. However, when ancillary departments like clinical laboratories, pharmacy, and radiology began to implement computer systems, the power relationships (and hence the politics) began to change. Ancillary departments are clinical in nature and therefore the department heads are clinicians—pathologists, pharmacists and radiologists. They became not only the primary customers of IT departments but took on the responsibility of deciding the requirements definitions for the systems they wanted to use in their own departments.

In the 1990s, there were a wide variety of "departmental" systems available on the market, although as we have seen, few standards for interoperability among these systems. The result was what came to be known as "best of breed" strategies as clinicians used their expertise about departmental operations to select what they felt was the best computer system for their department. The fact that these systems had different hardware and operating system configurations from each other and were often developed in specialized coding languages, were less important than the fact that they met the requirements that the clinical department heads stipulated. In this process, IT investments became more political as clinical departments challenged the decisions that had historically been made by the IT leadership and the executive leaderships—who were most often not clinically trained.

At about the same time, as we noted earlier, the 1991 publication *The Computer-Based Patient Record: An Essential Technology for Health Care* by the Institute of Medicine significantly elevated the visibility of IT investments supporting clinical care.[29] A little over a decade later, then President George W. Bush continued elevating the visibility of electronic medical records with his statement that he "believes that innovations in electronic health records and the secure exchange of medical information will help transform health care in America."[30] Bush's commitment was that by 2014, every American would have an electronic medical record.

Several years later, the American Recovery and Reinvestment Act of 2009 (ARRA)—contained more than $30 billion in financial incentives for physicians and hospitals to adopt electronic health records. At that point, with federal government financial incentives, IT investments in health care became very focused on clinical systems, and the politics within provider organizations began to change as well. Many created Chief Medical Information Officer (CMIO) positions, some reporting to CIOs, some reporting to other senior administrative positions, and some becoming CIOs with responsibility of all IT operations. Clinicians, some with backgrounds in computer science and others who subsequently became newly board certified in informatics,[31] began to emerge as leaders in the selection of electronic medical record (EMR) systems. The power relationships between clinicians and IT professionals were changing as well, as clinicians began to assert their influence over the EMR IT investments.

At the same time, companies selling computer systems to health care provider organizations began to consolidate and broaden their product suites. Epic, for example, which started by developing products for physician billing, gradually expanded their product suite to include capabilities for inpatient management and virtually all the ancillary departments (i.e., laboratories, pharmacy, and radiology). Cerner, Epic's main competitor, started with a suite of products for ancillary departments and expanded its own product line to include support for inpatient and outpatient activities. These developments effectively marked the end of the "best of breed" strategy that many provider organizations had been pursuing. "Single vendor" solutions became more important as vendors' product suites became more integrated and IT departments sought to reduce the complexity of their environments by reducing the number of vendors they had to engage.

Politics, both national and organizational, pervade much of the health care industry. In part, the intensity of both national and organizational politics is due to the enormous amount of money spent on health care at all levels of government and in the private sector (through employer-sponsored health programs), and to the fact that health care is itself so personal. Major legislative changes at the federal level bring out clear differences of ideology and opinion and can impact everyone who is now or is likely to become a patient.

Virtually all discussions about health care access, provision and payment since World War II have reflected a divide between Democrats and Republicans. The arguments on each side have essentially been drawn on what the appropriate role of the federal government should be and what role individual choice should have in purchasing health care insurance. Democrats are generally more comfortable with a major role for the government in assuring access to health care, providing health care services, and in paying for those services. Republicans, on the other hand, seek to limit the government's role (both federal and state) and prefer to let "market forces" determine who gets access, how services are provided and who pays for those services. So, the fundamental question becomes, "What role should free markets versus the government play in the access, provision and payment for health care services?"

Such questions cannot be answered by investments in information technology and indeed there is probably only a minimal role for IT in addressing these questions. They are in the realm of policy and political ideology. Even though IT can facilitate the collection, storage and management of clinical data, and likely facilitate the use of data essential for the creation of value-based care models, until there is general agreement among politicians and health care professionals on the need to proceed with developing and implementing such models, IT investments will remain on the side line.

The interweaving of IT investments with both national and organizational politics has been evolving for close to thirty years. In the process, hundreds of millions of dollars have been spent and the relationships among clinicians, politicians, IT professionals and provider executive have evolved as well. All of this has created a complex set of political relationships that appear to be quite different from what might be found in any other industry.

Notes

1. Politics, from Greek *Politiká*, definition: "affairs of the cities." "The activities of the government, members of law-making organizations, or people who try to influence the way a country is governed." Cambridge Dictionary. From https://dictionary.cambridge.org/dictionary/english/politics. (Accessed on June 17, 2018.)
2. Historically, state and local governments have played lesser roles than the federal government in the provision of health care services, especially with the passage of federal Medicare and Medicaid legislation in 1965.

3. Center for Medicare and Medicaid Services. https://www.cms.gov/research-statistics-data-and-systems/statistics-trends-and-reports/nationalhealthexpenddata/nhe-fact-sheet.html. (Accessed on June 17, 2018.)

4. Center for Medicare and Medicaid Services. https://www.cms.gov/research-statistics-data-and-systems/statistics-trends-and-reports/nationalhealthexpenddata/nhe-fact-sheet.html. (Accessed on June 17, 2018.)

5. Center for Medicare and Medicaid Services. https://www.cms.gov/About-CMS/Agency-information/History/ (Accessed on June 17, 2018.)

6. "Summary of the Affordable Care Act," Henry J. Kaiser Family Foundation, April 25, 2013. http://kff.org/health-reform/fact-sheet/summary-of-the-affordable-care-act/. (Accessed on June 17, 2018.)

7. "Summary of Coverage Provisions in the Patient Protection and Affordable Care Act," Henry J. Kaiser Family Foundation, July 17, 2012. http://kff.org/health-costs/issue-brief/summary-of-coverage-provisions-in-the-patient/. (Accessed on June 17, 2018.)

8. Chris Riotta, "GOP Aims to Kill Obamacare Yet Again After Failing 70 Times," *Newsweek*, July 29, 2017. http://www.newsweek.com/gop-health-care-bill-repeal-and-replace-70-failed-attempts-643832. (Accessed on June 17, 2018.)

9. Although the Republicans failed in their attempts to overturn Obamacare legislation, they have been more successful with smaller measures such as the repeal of the individual mandate, the elimination of the Medicare Cost Control Board, permitting health insurance plans with less coverage and higher deductibles, elimination of the federal government's participation in the cost sharing reduction subsidies. See https://www.nytimes.com/2018/03/12/opinion/republicans-obamacare-health-care.html. (Accessed on June 17, 2018.)

10. Andy Slavitt, "The Republican Cold War on the Affordable Care Act," Vox, May 14, 2018. https://www.vox.com/the-big-idea/2018/5/14/17350818/affordable-care-act-repeal-attacks-gop-medicaid-preexisting-condition-health. (Accessed on August 24, 2018.) See also Julie Rovner, "Timeline: Despite GOP's Failure to Repeal Obamacare, the ACA Has Changed Kaiser Health," *The Washington Post*, April 5, 2018. https://www.washingtonpost.com/national/health-science/timeline-despite-gops-failure-to-repeal-obamacare-the-aca-has-changed/2018/04/05/

dba36240-38b1-11e8-af3c-2123715f78df_story.
html?noredirect=on&utm_term=.cada1e272ddb. (Accessed on
August 24, 2018.)

11. "Commonwealth Fund Affordable Care Act Tracking Survey,
February to March 2018," Commonwealth Fund, May 1,
2018. https://www.commonwealthfund.org/publications/sur-
veys/2018/may/commonwealth-fund-affordable-care-act-track-
ing-survey-february-march. (Accessed on August 24, 2018.)

12. See, for example, *The Washington Post*, https://www.wash-
ingtonpost.com/blogs/fact-checker/post/how-many-pages-of-
regulations-for-obamacare/2013/05/14/61eec914-bcf9-11e2-9b09-
1638acc3942e_blog.html?utm_term=.5029a0b8292d. (Accessed
on June 17, 2018.) Also, see Rob Schwab, https://robschwab.
com/how-many-pages-is-obamacare/ for some of the complexities of counting pages. (Accessed on June 17, 2018.)

13. Rob Schwab, "How Many Pages Is Obamacare?" March 1,
2016. https://robschwab.com/how-many-pages-is-obamacare/.
(Accessed on June 17, 2018.)

14. For an in depth discussion of these factors, see "Why
Republicans Hate Obamacare," *The Economist*, December
11, 2016. http://www.economist.com/blogs/economist-
explains/2016/12/economist-explains-1. (Accessed on
June 17, 2018.)

15. See, for example, a CNN news report: https://www.cnn.
com/2017/12/08/opinions/paul-ryan-delivers-the-ugly-news-on-
medicare-louis/index.html. (Accessed on June 17, 2018.)

16. "ARRA Economic Stimulus Package," HITECH Answers. http://
www.hitechanswers.net/about/about-arra/. (Accessed on June
17, 2018.)

17. To reiterate an endnote in Chapter 2, Electronic Health
Record (EHR) Systems and Electronic Medical Record (EMR)
Systems are often used interchangeably. Some argue that
EHRs are a somewhat broader concept, embracing any
health-related data whether from a physician encounter, a
hospital stay, patient-initiated comments or observations, data
from wearables, etc., while an EMR is a somewhat narrower
concept, and typically includes only data that is collected
during a physician encounter or an inpatient stay. In practice, these distinctions are often lost and the terms are used
interchangeably.

18. Centers for Medicare and Medicaid Services. https://www.cms.gov/research-statistics-data-and-systems/statistics-trends-and-reports/nationalhealthexpenddata/nhe-fact-sheet.html. (Accessed on June 17, 2018.)

19. Opinionator, *The New York Times*, March 16, 2013. https://opinionator.blogs.nytimes.com/2013/03/16/healing-the-hospital-hierarchy/. (Accessed on June 17, 2018.) See also M. M. Walton, "Hierarchies: the Berlin Wall of Patient Safety," *Qual Saf Health Care.* 2006 Aug; 15(4): 229–230. U.S. National Library of Medicine National Institutes of Health. https://www.ncbi.nlm.nih.gov/pmc/articles/PMC2564017/. (Accessed on June 17, 2018.) See also Advisory Board. https://www.advisory.com/Daily-Briefing/2013/03/18/Brown-The-hospital-hierarchy-needs-reform. (Accessed on June 17, 2018.)

20. Chapter 3 noted that in 2016, physician practice ownership dropped below 50% for the first time and the percentage of physicians employed by hospitals grew by 34% between 2000 and 2010.

21. Brent C. James and Gregory P. Poulsen, "The Case for Capitation," *Harvard Business Review,* July–August 2016. https://hbr.org/2016/07/the-case-for-capitation. (Accessed on June 17, 2018.)

22. "Updated Physician Practice Acquisition Study: National and Regional Changes in Physician Employment 2012–2016," Physicians Advocacy Institute. http://www.physiciansadvocacy-institute.org/PAI-Research/Physician-Employment. (Accessed on June 17, 2018.)

23. Jenny Gold, "Accountable Care Organizations, Explained," National Public Radio, January 18, 2011. http://www.npr.org/2011/04/01/132937232/accountable-care-organizations-explained. (Accessed on June 17, 2018.)

24. Evaluation and Management Services are essential physician/patient encounters that focus on history, examination process, and complexity of medical decision making. See Modern Medicine Network. http://medicaleconomics.modernmedicine.com/medical-economics/RC/evaluation-and-management-bill-correct-level-care. (Accessed on June 17, 2018.)

25. Payment increases in shifting from physician office rates to hospital rates range from 30% for E&M services to 77% for cardiac imaging. Avalere Health. http://go.avalere.com/acton/att

achment/12909/f-0298/1/-/-/-/-/20160212%20-%20Payment%20
Differentials%20Across%20Settings%20White%20Paper_FINAL.
pdf. (Accessed on June 17, 2018.)

26. A Diagnosis-Related Group (DRG) is a statistical system of classifying any inpatient stay into groups for the purposes of payment. The DRG classification system divides possible diagnoses into more than 20 major body systems and subdivides them into almost 500 groups for the purpose of Medicare reimbursement. See American Health Lawyers Association. https://www.healthlawyers.org/hlresources/Health%20Law%20Wiki/Diagnosis-related%20group%20(DRG).aspx. (Accessed on June 17, 2018.)

27. When a patient is admitted to a hospital, the admitting physician assigns an "admitting diagnosis" which equates to one of the codes contained within the DRG coding manual. Payment for the patient's stay is determined by this DRG, in most cases regardless of what happens to the patient subsequently. In effect, the hospital bears the financial risk for any subsequent complications the patient may experience.

28. See, for example, Centers for Medicare and Medicaid Services. https://www.cms.gov/Medicare/Quality-Initiatives-Patient-Assessment-Instruments/Value-Based-Programs/Value-Based-Programs.html and https://www.cms.gov/Newsroom/MediaReleaseDatabase/Fact-sheets/2015-Fact-sheets-items/2015-08-13-2.html. (Accessed on June 17, 2018.)

29. Richard S. Dick, Elaine B. Steen, and Don E. Detmer, eds, *The Computer-Based Patient Record: An Essential Technology for Health Care*, Revised Edition, Institute of Medicine, 1997. https://www.nap.edu/catalog/5306/the-computer-based-patient-record-an-essential-technology-for-health. (Accessed on June 17, 2018.)

30. "President Bush Continues EHR Push, Sets National Goals," Healthcare IT News, April 26, 2004. http://www.healthcare-itnews.com/news/president-bush-continues-ehr-push-sets-national-goals. (Accessed on June 17, 2018.)

31. A formal board certification in Clinical Informatics was officially approved by the American Board of Preventive Medicine in September 2011. For a history, see American Medical Informatics Association. https://www.amia.org/clinical-informatics-board-review-course/history. (Accessed on June 17, 2018.)

Chapter 10

How Health Care Markets and Payments Work ... or Don't!

10.1 Introduction

The health care marketplace in the United States appears to perform in ways that are simply not predictable according to classic economic theories. Assumptions about the behavior of suppliers and customers that are engrained in economic and business models about how corporate America works (or is supposed to work) seem not to apply to the health care marketplace. This can have a significant impact on policies and programs, as well as on the creation, sale and implementation of information technology (IT) in health care. This chapter explores some of the issues that arise from the inapplicability of common business principles to health care industry markets, payments and prices.

Chapter 2 introduced the notion that the fundamental transaction in health care services is that which takes place between the clinician and the patient. This transaction is analogous to what is typically referred to as a *basic business transaction*, that is, the interaction that takes place between a seller and a buyer in any marketplace. Economists use descriptions of this type of transaction as the basis for defining markets. When a seller and a buyer come together and agree on a price for what the seller is offering to the buyer, they can say that a "market has been made."[1]

Typically, buyers seek a product or service from a supplier, agreeing to exchange a certain amount of money (or in a barter economy, goods may be substituted for money) in return for receiving the service or product offered by a supplier.[2] At its simplest, this type of business transaction is straightforward and defines the foundation of what has taken place between buyers and sellers in commercial markets for centuries.

A simplified version of the most basic market model is provided in Figure 10.1.

For a market to be described as "efficient," the seller must have a clear idea of what s/he is willing to accept in exchange for providing the product or service, and the buyer must be fully informed of the nature of the product or service being offered. In other words, there should not be any secrets as to what the seller expects from the exchange and the buyer

Figure 10.1 Basic market exchange model.

should be provided with a full and accurate description of the nature of the product or service being offered.

In theory, efficient markets are best because: (1) no resources are wasted when the seller gets what is deemed a "fair" price, that is, the price at which the seller is willing to part with his/her goods or services; and (2) the buyer has full knowledge of what s/he is getting and willingly gives up resources in exchange for the product or service being offered and therefore does not waste resources on a product or service that is not wanted, needed, or comes with hidden side effects.

In practice, this fundamental assumption about "full disclosure" by both the seller and the buyer can be violated. In the contract (whether written or verbal) between the seller and the buyer, there may be "hidden fees" that are not fully disclosed at the time of the transaction, or the buyer may not be fully aware of uncertainties regarding the quality of the product or service being acquired. In fact, both concerns at times plague the markets for health care products and services—the seller (e.g., a clinician, hospital, or pharmaceutical company) may not fully disclose the price (especially if payment is through a third party) and the buyer (e.g., the patient) may not have full information regarding the service s/he is receiving (e.g., the quality of the care being provided). So even at the outset, there are challenges to assuming that the market for health care services is at all efficient.[3]

10.2 Third-Party Payers

Business transactions come with the assumption that the seller is the one specifically providing the product or service, the buyer has the resources at his or her disposal to exchange for the product or service being offered, and that the price paid for the acquired product or service is established through this transaction process and is known or transparent to the buyer and the seller. Much of the economic activity that takes place in America every day follows this model—but not in health care.

The fundamental health care services transaction typically involves an additional role that complicates the simplicity of the roles of seller and buyer, a role often referred to as the "third-party payer." In health care the assumption that the buyer (i.e., the patient) has the resources on their own to compensate the seller (i.e., the clinician) for their services does not hold. In fact, the federal government's 2016 report on National Health Expenditures indicates that households covered only 28.1% of all health care expenditures directly, while the federal government provided 28.3%, private business (largely through insurance premium payments) 19.9%, and state and local governments 16.9%.[4]

Third-party payments dominate health care, and the role of private companies in providing health insurance is unique in the United States. According to 2015 data from the 34-member Organization for Economic Co-operation and Development (OECD), the United States has substantially more private insurance coverage than any other country. Private insurance covers 0.3% of the population in Iceland, 0.8% in Spain, 10.8% in Germany, 18.8% in Chile, and 55.3% in the United States. Approximately 85% of OECD countries cover their entire population through publicly funding insurance payment programs.[5] Any consideration to changing the current structure of third-party payers must consider the extraordinary role that private companies play in America's health insurance marketplace.[6]

The health care services received by individuals can be expensive, episodic and often unpredictable, so some type of insurance program to manage the risk of these events makes sense. Similar to insurance for homes and automobiles, collecting premium payments and then pooling them across a large population for later payment of claims helps individuals manage the risk of health care adversity. However, in most industries which supply products or services, insurance payments are not the most common way of paying for the receipt of products or services.

In health care services transactions, the buyer (i.e., the patient) does not provide the resources in exchange for the health care services provided in almost 75% of the payment transactions that take place. This simply does not happen in any other industry in our economy. If you do not have the resources to acquire the product or service, you go without. But to go without health care when you most need it can be a life-limiting decision.

Figure 10.2 illustrates the complexity that health care third-party payments bring to the basic market model.

In Figure 10.2, the clinician provides health care services to the patient. As a result of this encounter, the clinician submits a claim to a third-party payer (which could be a government agency or an insurance company). The payer reviews the claim and then if determined to be appropriate and consistent with the terms of their contractual relationship, sends a payment. As if this process were not complicated enough, there are additional challenges arising from requirements in specific situations such as co-payments, deductibles, caps, lifetime benefit restrictions, etc. Figure 10.2 also illustrates that the third-party payer can for a number of reasons reject the

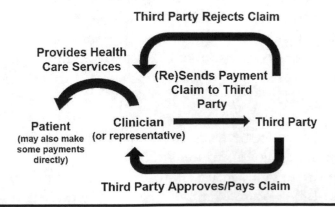

Figure 10.2   Basic market model applied to health care.

claim submitted by the provider—justification for the claim is incomplete, data are missing, claim submitted after a contractual deadline, processing errors on the part of the provider or the payer, etc. If the provider thinks that the claim should still be paid, it might be submitted again for payment with corrections, in some cases substantially lengthening the time between when the service is rendered, the claim submitted, and the claim paid. The major point beyond the complexity of claims processing generally, and the major departure from a "normal" economic market model, is that payment to the seller (the clinician as provider) comes not from the buyer (the patient) but from an essentially uninvolved third party.

This poses an interesting question: who is "making the market" in health care services? In most cases it is not the provider and the patient (even though they are essential to the transaction), but a "third-party payer" that actually "makes the market."[7]

Third-party payments have not always been the standard in the health care industry. Prior to World War II, payments to physicians were typically made directly by the patients themselves—anecdotes are common about payments being made through bartering. The creation of a formal insurance model for health care payments started with the Blue Cross Association, which in 1929 provided benefits for hospital care in return for monthly payments from participants. Blue Shield, which provided payments to physicians, was created in 1939 and followed a similar business model.[8]

During World War II, the federal government instigated wage and price controls in an effort to avoid the hyperinflation that occurred in Germany after World War I. As indicated in one recent account,

> In reaction to the wage controls, many labor groups planned to go on strike *en masse*. In order to avert the strike, in a concession to the labor groups, the War Labor Board exempted employer-paid health benefits from wage controls and income tax. ... This

historical accident created a tax advantage that drove enormous demand for employer-provided health insurance plans over the previously more common individual health insurance. Employers received a 100% tax deduction while the benefits employees received were exempt from federal, state, and city taxation.[9]

In 1945, President Truman proposed a nationalized health care program, with five major components[10]:

1. Construction of high quality, modern hospitals
2. Development of public health services, both to control the spread of infectious diseases and improve sanitary conditions across the nation, and to improve maternal and child health care
3. Increase in the nation's investment in medical research and education
4. Development of a "national health insurance program" for everyone
5. Implementation of a national program of cash assistance for those who became ill or injured to replace income lost

The proposals for a national health insurance program and cash assistance brought an almost immediate reaction from the American Medical Association, which was soon joined by more than 1,800 other organizations including the American Bar Association, the American Legion and the American Farm Bureau Federation. The groups railed against "socialized medicine," which in a time of anti-communist fervor, stalled efforts in Congress to pass legislation to enact Truman's proposals.[11]

What remained in place, however, were the tax advantages to employers and employees for employer-paid health insurance premiums, and the pattern and principle of third-party payments for health care become firmly ensconced in nation's economy and culture.

Twenty years later, Lyndon Johnson's successful efforts to enact Medicare and Medicaid legislation to provide health care payments for the elderly and those living in poverty provided some financial payment for those who were not working. However, both Medicare and Medicaid continued the third-party payment model, with the federal government replacing private employers as the "third party." (See Chapter 9 for discussion regarding the political aspects of health care insurance programs.)

Despite these programs, the number of uninsured families and individuals remained at significant levels. The Census Bureau's 2011 Current Population Survey identified close to 50 million individuals or about 16.3% of the population as uninsured.[12] The problem with an uninsured population is that even minor ailments end up being treated in emergency rooms (which are not designed for minor treatments) and if hospitalized, these patients end up not being able to pay for their care. The result is that hospitals bear the cost in both situations, essentially providing highly costly care, or care without being paid at all. In addition, individuals who carry no health insurance are more likely to go without needed preventive care, and typically do not seek care for either major or chronic conditions. In many situations, the cost of insurance premiums is simply too great for those with low incomes.[13]

The Accountable Care Act of 2008 (ACA) sought to increase access and to reduce the number of uninsured individuals and families through expanded Medicaid coverage and by subsidizing the costs of care for those with limited incomes, enabling them to purchase health care insurance from private insurance companies through market exchanges set up by federal and state governments. By the end of 2016, the overall number of uninsured had been reduced from 16% of the population in 2010 to 11%.

Models for third-party payments seem to work well during times in which health costs increase minimally or at least in predictable ways, and the economy is growing so that employee earnings rise over time along with government revenues. Insurance companies can then increase the premiums paid by their customers to cover the claims filed for payment and earn a profit margin as well. A rise in government payments may also be manageable as long as revenues increase.

10.3 Costs

Over the past 50 years, health care costs as a percentage of the Gross Domestic Product (GDP) have increased each year, in effect consuming more and more of what the economy produces (see Figure 10.3). The U.S. Bureau of Labor Statistics has stated that consumer spending for health care increased

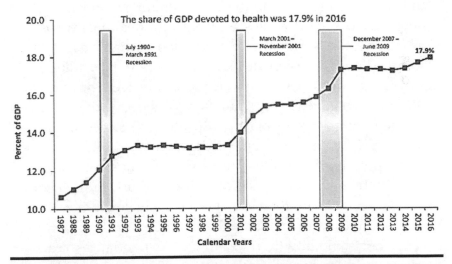

Figure 10.3 **National health expenditures as percent of gross domestic product. (From https://www.cms.gov/Research-Statistics-Data-and-Systems/Statistics-Trends-and-Reports/NationalHealthExpendData/Downloads/NHE-Presentation-Slides.pdf. Data for this figure was sourced from the Centers for Medicare & Medicaid Services, Office of the Actuary, National Health Statistics Group and the U.S. Department of Commerce, Bureau of Economic Analysis and National Bureau of Economic Research, Inc. Accessed on June 19, 2018.)**

by more than 60% between 1984 and 2014, while expenditures for food, transportation, and apparel and services each decreased by at least 10%.[14]

If this trend continues, federal expenditures on health care alone could approach 50% of the country's GDP by 2050, potentially crowding out expenditures for just about everything else, including defense and education.[15]

Insurance companies, in an effort to manage their increasing financial risk, have shifted some of these rising costs to providers and patients. They began to require higher deductibles before an insurance payment occurred, refused to cover certain medical conditions and lowered the amount they would pay or at times outright refused to pay for a particular visit, procedure or hospital stay. "Pre-certification or pre-authorization," in which a payer's approval was required before a patient could seek care, became common practice—the lack of prior approval or authorization could result in the denial of any payment.

Many factors are driving the increase in health care costs year over year.[16] These include a population that is aging (as older people generally incur more health care expenditures than younger ones), recent government subsidies through the ACA that have increased the numbers of those with access to care, the falling share of personal health care expenditures paid directly by patients,[17] and what might be termed "unnecessary" spending for health care services.[18] These increases were abated somewhat by the overall downturn in the economy that occurred in 2008 and the relatively small increases in overall economic growth since then.

The consistent growth in health care expenditures year over year and the overall size of the industry make health care one of the most important drivers of the American economy. However, as was noted earlier, virtually unchecked growth can have significant consequences. The past several years of increasing costs have produced a very challenging environment for insurance companies. In order to keep pace with increasing costs, for example, they created High Deductible

Health Plans (HDHP), which are insurance plans with lower premiums but higher deductibles (and often less coverage) than more traditional health insurance plans.[19] Such plans are designed to shift more of the cost burden onto the patients who must pay more out of their pockets before any insurance payments are made. Since 2009, the average deductible under HDHPs has increased almost 90%. This is part of a general trend that has seen consumer out-of-pocket spending for health care increase by 46% between 2014 and what is projected for 2019.[20]

10.4 Prices

There are many ways to think about the concept of "price," whether it be an "asking price," a "selling price," a "bid price" or a "transaction price"—in fact there is an entire branch of microeconomics that focuses on "price theory."[21] But a fundamental definition of price is

> Price is the amount that a seller and a buyer agree is appropriate for goods and/or services to be provided by the seller in return for some form of payment (which could be goods in a barter arrangement or currency in a cash transaction) by the buyer.

Intuitively this makes sense even in simple cases. A grocery store customer wishes to purchase a pound of meat. The grocery store has decided that they will provide the meat to the buyer in exchange for $5.99 per pound in currency issued by the U.S. government. So, we would say that the "price" is $5.99 per pound. In this example, the customer knows the "price" of the meat since it is typically stamped on a label affixed to the package. This is admittedly a simple case where the seller's price is transparent to the buyer and in most cases the grocery store will not negotiate a lower price even if requested to do so by the customer. The buyer also assumes that the characteristics of the meat being sold are apparent, whether prime or choice grade, 75% lean or 85% lean, grass fed or not, etc. In more complex situations, such as purchasing an automobile, the buyer in many cases can negotiate a lower price from the seller to complete the transaction, e.g., by using cost information provided by numerous third parties.

In the health care industry, decisions about pricing are much more complex. First, we have already established that the buyer (the patient) and the seller (the clinician or hospital) do not negotiate directly on the price of the services being provided, due to the presence of third-party payers. Second, in most cases the buyer has no idea of the costs for these services. Third, the amount of payments from third parties to clinicians and hospitals is often negotiated based less on actual cost than on other factors, e.g., how many patients are likely to be seen, demonstrated care management through metrics such as average length of stay in the hospital, number of re-admissions for the same diagnosis, etc.

10.5 A Fundamental Principle of Insurance

Third-party payers, whether public or private, operate under a principle fundamental to any insurance program: the amount of premiums paid in must equal at least the amount of the claims paid out over some specific time period. Quite simply, if the amount of claims paid out exceeds the amount of premiums paid in, the program will go bankrupt. Private insurance companies' profit margins are based in part on the difference between people who pay premiums and do not file claims and those who pay premiums and do file claims.[22]

When the Affordable Care Act (ACA) was introduced, a new type of market mechanism was created, the "Exchange Markets." While the federal government was willing to subsidize premium payments for those at or near the official poverty line, it also required that both younger (and therefore presumably healthier) individuals and employers with a certain number of employees, pay insurance premiums. This provision, known as the "individual mandate"—was intended to provide some balance between premiums paid in and claims paid out. Healthier individuals paying premiums but not filing claims are needed to balance individuals who were less healthy and therefore would file more claims.

The Affordable Care Act was created to expand health insurance coverage to historically uninsured or under insured members of the population, and overall to both expand health insurance coverage and to make it more affordable to certain members of the population. In addition, it required that health care insurance policies cover pre-existing conditions, cover dependents until the age of 26, provide preventive care without cost sharing, and meet certain requirements for coverage and deductibles. It also required that larger employers provide affordable, comprehensive health insurance to full-time employees (also called the employer mandate). While not addressing health care costs directly, the ACA sought to expand insurance coverage and to make health care insurance more affordable for those at the lower end of the income ladder.

The "individual mandate" became a major issue for Republicans in the Congress, who argued that no one should be required to purchase health care insurance if they did not want to. In other words, everyone should have a choice about whether to participate in the market for health care insurance. The problem with this approach is that it violates a fundamental insurance principle by leaving out of the program generally healthy individuals whose premium payments (and limited claims) could be used to support those who were more likely to make claims (e.g., those living in or near poverty levels and the elderly, both of whom historically have had greater health care expenses).

10.6 Measuring Value in Health Care Markets

Another way to look at the markets in health care is to focus on what economists call the "value proposition"—in the most general terms, value equates to the benefits that a consumer perceives to accrue from participating in a particular transaction.

In most economic transactions, and for markets to work efficiently, the value proposition of the seller and that of the buyer (i.e., the benefits that each perceive to stem from the transaction) must be aligned. In "normal" market situations, the seller offers goods or services which are valued by the buyer, and the buyer provides payment in some form in exchange for the seller's goods or services. Thus, the value proposition for the seller (receiving compensation in exchange for providing a good or service) aligns with that of the buyer (who provides resources in exchange for receiving the goods or services offered by the seller). With the third-party payment model so pervasive in the health care industry, this alignment of value propositions between seller and buyer does not exist. The overall size of health care spending in the United States might be more tolerable (although certainly not if spending continues at the current rate) if there was a sense that the country was actually "getting its money's worth" from the health care industry. In fact, one survey claimed that 75% of Americans think that they do not get the value they expect from the money they spend.[23]

Recent statistics document this concern. Consider the following:

- The United States has higher per capita health care expenditures than other countries.[24]
- The United States has fewer per capita hospital and physician visits than other countries.
- In comparison to adults in the other 10 countries, adults in the United States tend to be sicker and more economically disadvantaged.[25]

- Infant mortality rates are better in 15 other countries.[26]
- Life expectancy at birth is lower in the United States than in 10 other comparable countries.[27]

The third-party payment model has introduced a complexity into health care markets and payments that has in many ways failed to support the delivery of quality health care at affordable prices. As noted above, by some measures the quality of health care currently being provided in the United States ranks significantly behind other countries, and payers are constantly seeking to shift the financial risk associated with health care delivery to both patients and providers. Certainly, in terms of receiving value for the money spent, one would have to conclude that this is not working well—for payers, for providers or for patients.

In addition, the physician as seller and patient as buyer is a simplification of the complexity of the environment in which health care services are delivered and the multiple persons, departments and organizations that are often involved in providing a clinical service to a patient. Payments may need to be made to any or all these individuals or organizations even if the actual transaction occurs in a single setting.[28]

10.7 The Move toward Value-Based Care

Michael Porter, in his book, *Redefining Health Care*,[29] argues that the most important strategy for containing health care costs and addressing the challenges of providing high quality health care is to focus on delivering better outcomes for patients at the lowest possible cost. Porter's premise has become the foundation for a focus not just on lowering costs or shifting financial risk, but on the overall effort to provide "value-based care" (VBC). Value-based care focuses specifically on patient outcomes versus simply counting visits and procedures, which is the basis of historical "fee-for-service" models. The shift to

VBC has been underway with efforts by the federal government going back almost 30 years, unfortunately without much demonstrable success—attesting again to the complexity that plagues the health care industry. The intention over time is to provide reimbursement for how well hospitals and physicians perform in terms of the outcomes of their patients (i.e., providing "value-based" purchasing rather than "volume" based purchasing) rather than simply counting visits and procedures.[30]

IT investments will be expected to play a major role in this transition, even while many acknowledge the difficulty with measuring the value of these transactions in the first place. For example, companies have created new IT investment opportunities in analytics, seeking to capitalize on this coming transition. Analytics for the most part rely on a solid foundation of clinical data to provide both baseline and accumulated clinical data on which to make judgments about the impact of various clinical interventions.[31] This will require a continuing focus on IT investments, since absent IT capabilities, the opportunities for the collection, management and analysis of large clinical data sets will simply not exist. (The challenges with the complexity of clinical data are discussed in Chapter 6.)

High quality clinical care, even with all the current challenges to measuring "quality" accurately and meaningfully, is essential to everyone involved in the business of health care, including hospitals, health systems, payers, companies providing IT systems, physicians, and patients. There is no exclusive ownership of these challenges as it will take coordination and teamwork among all players to realize the IT investment returns that need to come from the choices being made.

One of the more recent initiatives by the federal government to continue to shift financial risk while emphasizing a greater focus on quality has been with the initiation of "bundled payments":

> Under a bundled payment model, providers and/or healthcare facilities are paid a single payment for all

the services performed to treat a patient undergoing a specific episode of care. An "episode of care" is the care delivery process for a certain condition or care delivered within a defined period of time.[32]

Bundled payments for orthopedic procedures were initially announced by the federal government in mid-2015,[33] and implemented in April 2016. Cardiac bundles were scheduled for a 2018 implementation. Private insurers are understandably supporting these types of efforts to control health care costs.[34] However, in August 2017, the Department of Health and Human Services announced the elimination of mandatory bundled payment programs, preferring to let such initiatives proceed on a voluntary basis. This is generally consistent with the ideological view that cost saving programs in health care should follow the same market-driven models found in private business.[35]

While one might think it difficult to argue against providers taking on more financial risk for the care they provide and as well an interest in attempting to define and reward higher quality services, there are detractors to this process. The arguments that were made against the ACA when it was initially proposed continue today, especially the requirement for mandatory participation in new payment models developed by the federal government. In addition, in the continuing move toward VBC, there are additional requirements for documentation and reporting that fall largely on the clinicians. It is likely that information technology investments may be able to alleviate some of the documentation burden, although today's EMRs still require a significant amount of data entry by clinicians.

It remains the fundamental fact that in health care, patients as customers typically pay for only a portion of the cost of the services they receive. In every other industry, customers are expected at some point to pay for the products they purchase and the services they use, whether at the

time of purchase or through some type of extended payment arrangement. With extensive third-party involvement in
the payment process, however, the management of cost will
remain a significant contributing factor to the complexity of
the health care industry.

Notes

1. For a brief but good description of markets, see Investopedia.
   http://www.investopedia.com/terms/m/market.asp. (Accessed
   on June 17, 2018.)
2. The exchange between supplier and customer is technically
   an exchange of resources, which can take many forms as
   long as the buyer and the seller agree on the value of what is
   being exchanged—e.g., a trade of goods for services, a barter
   in which specific goods are exchanged or using some form of
   currency to compensate the supplier for the products or services provided. In our discussion we are assuming that what
   is being supplied is a specific health care service and that the
   customer is the patient, and in most cases, currency was used
   to complete the transaction although, as we will see, this currency does not always come directly from the customer—a
   distinctly non-traditional business model.
3. Much of federal government regulation is directed to responding to these challenges. For example, the FDA has extensive
   regulations regarding how the efficacy of drugs must be demonstrated prior to sale, and recent efforts by U.S. Health and
   Human Services to move toward value-based care have focused
   on attempting to document the quality of clinical care.
4. Centers for Medicare and Medicaid, "National Health Expenditures,
   2016 Highlights." https://www.cms.gov/research-statistics-data-and-
   systems/statistics-trends-and-reports/nationalhealthexpenddata/
   downloads/highlights.pdf. (Accessed on June 17, 2018.)
5. Organization for Economic Cooperation and Development,
   "Health at a Glance 2017: OECD Indicators." https://read.
   oecd-ilibrary.org/social-issues-migration-health/health-at-a-
   glance-2017/population-coverage-for-a-core-set-of-services-
   2015-or-nearest-year_health_glance-2017-graph52-en#page1.
   (Accessed on June 17, 2018.)

6. Recent proposals from a number of politicians for a "single payer" health insurance program in the United States (often referred to as "Medicare for all") typically do not consider the impact on the substantial private companies that now provide health insurance coverage.

7. This situation has evolved as the Republican-controlled Congress has worked to limit what the federal government pays for health care services and as insurance companies increase copayments and deductible limits through so called "High Deductible Health Plans." In both the underlying motivation is to shift the cost of health care services more directly to those who use those services, i.e., the patients.

8. For more information on Blue Cross Blue Shield's history, see https://www.bcbs.com/the-health-of-america/articles/health-insurance-invention-innovation-history-blue-cross-and-blue. (Accessed on June 17, 2018.)

9. Rick Lindquist, "Part 1: The History of U.S. Employer-Provided Health Insurance—Post-World War II," *PeopleKeep*, June 5, 2014. https://www.zanebenefits.com/blog/part-1-the-history-of-u.s.-employer-provided-health-insurance-post-world-war-ii. (Accessed on June 17, 2018.)

10. PBS News Hour, "69 Years Ago, a President Pitches His Idea for National Health Care," November 19, 2014. http://www.pbs.org/newshour/updates/november-19-1945-harry-truman-calls-national-health-insurance-program/. (Accessed on June 17, 2018.)

11. PBS News Hour, "69 Years Ago, a President Pitches His Idea for National Health Care," November 19, 2014. http://www.pbs.org/newshour/updates/november-19-1945-harry-truman-calls-national-health-insurance-program/. (Accessed on June 17, 2018.)

12. "Overview of the Uninsured in the United States: A Summary of the 2011 Current Population Survey," U.S. Department of Health and Human Services, September 13, 2011. https://aspe.hhs.gov/basic-report/overview-uninsured-united-states-summary-2011-current-population-survey. (Accessed on June 17, 2018.)

13. Henry J. Kaiser Foundation, "Key Facts about the Uninsured Population," September 19, 2017. https://www.kff.org/uninsured/fact-sheet/key-facts-about-the-uninsured-population/. (Accessed on June 19, 2018.)

14. TED, The Economics Daily, "Share of Total Spending on Healthcare Increased from 5 Percent in 1984 to 8 Percent in 2014," June 1, 2016. https://www.bls.gov/opub/ted/2016/share-of-total-spending-on-healthcare-increased-from-5-percent-in-1984-to-8-percent-in-2014.htm. (Accessed on June 19, 2018.)

15. Congressional Budget Office, "The Long Term Outlook for Health Care Spending," November 2007. https://www.cbo.gov/sites/default/files/110th-congress-2007-2008/reports/11-13-lt-health.pdf, p. 13. (Accessed on June 17, 2018.)

16. Kaiser Family Foundation, "Health Care Costs: A Primer," 2012, pp. 25–26. https://www.kff.org/health-costs/issue-brief/health-care-costs-a-primer/. (Accessed on June 19, 2018.)

17. Between 1970 and 2010, the share of personal health expenditures paid directly out-of-pocket by consumers fell from 40% to 14%. "Health Care Costs: A Primer," Kaiser Family Foundation, 2012, p. 25. https://www.kff.org/health-costs/issue-brief/health-care-costs-a-primer/. (Accessed on June 19, 2018.)

18. Some have estimated that 20% or more of total health care expenditures are due to various forms of waste, including overtreatment, failures of care coordination, failures of care delivery, administrative complexity, pricing failures, and fraud and abuse. See Donald M. Berwick and Andrew D. Hackbarth, "Eliminating Waste in U.S. Health Care," JAMA Online, March 14, 2012, pp. E1–E4, cited in "Health Care Costs: A Primer," Kaiser Family Foundation, 2012. https://www.kff.org/health-costs/issue-brief/health-care-costs-a-primer/ (Accessed on June 19, 2018.)

19. Such plans have been pejoratively labeled as "junk insurance."

20. Instamed, "Trends in Healthcare Payments Eighth Annual Report: 2017," May 2018. https://www.instamed.com/blog/trends-in-healthcare-seventh-annual-report-2016/. (Accessed on June 12, 2018.)

21. See, for example, Milton Friedman, *Price Theory*, originally published by Aldine de Gruter in 1962, and recently re-published by Transaction Publishing, New Brunswick, NJ, and London (2007).

22. In practice, the premiums to claims ratio is more complicated. Since premiums are paid before claims are filed, the insurance company in effect retains a reserve against future claims and often invests this reserve in assets that generate additional

returns. So, the margin for an insurance company is not simply the difference between premiums received and claims paid, but also includes income from investing the reserve.

23. Instamed, "Trends in Healthcare Payments Eighth Annual Report: 2017." https://www.instamed.com/blog/trends-in-health-care-seventh-annual-report-2016/. (Accessed on June 13, 2018.)

24. David Squires, "U.S. Health Care from a Global Perspective: Spending, Use of Services, Prices, and Health in 13 Countries," The Commonwealth Fund, October 8, 2015. http://www.com-monwealthfund.org/publications/issue-briefs/2015/oct/us-health-care-from-a-global-perspective. (Accessed on June 19, 2018.)

25. Robin Osborn, et al., "In New Survey of Eleven Countries, U.S. Adults Still Struggle with Access to and Affordability of Health Care," Health Affairs, December 2016. http://content.healthaf-fairs.org/content/early/2016/11/14/hlthaff.2016.1088. (Accessed on June 19, 2018.)

26. Aaron E. Carroll, "The U.S. Is Failing in Infant Mortality, Starting at One Month Old," *The New York Times*, June 6, 2016. https://www.nytimes.com/2016/06/07/upshot/the-us-is-failing-in-infant-mortality-starting-at-one-month-old.html?_r=0. (Accessed on June 19, 2018.)

27. Selena Gonzales and Bradley Sawyer, "How Does U.S. Life Expectancy Compare to Other Countries?" Peterson-Kaiser Health System Tracker, May 22, 2017. http://www.healthsystemtracker.org/chart-collection/u-s-life-expectancy-compare-countries/?_sf_s=life#item-u-s-lowest-life-expectancy-birth-among-comparable-countries. (Accessed on June 19, 2018.)

28. For example, a surgical procedure may take place at a single point in time (a transaction) but multiple providers may need to be paid. This could include not only the surgeon, but the operating room technicians and nurses, the anesthesiologist, pathologists examining excised tissue, as well as the organiza-tion in which the operation took place.

29. Michael E. Porter and Elizabeth Olmsted Teisberg, *Redefining Health Care: Creating Value-based Competition on Results.* Cambridge, MA: Harvard University Press, 2006.

30. "Better Care. Smarter Spending. Healthier People: Paying Providers for Value, Not Volume," Centers for Medicare and Medicaid Services. http://www.cms.gov/Newsroom/MediaReleaseDatabase/Fact-sheets/2015-Fact-sheets-items/2015-01-26-3.html. (Accessed on June 19, 2018.)

31. We referred to "big data" and "analytics" and population health in general in Chapter 4.

32. Jacqueline LaPointe, "Understanding the Basics of Bundled Payments in Healthcare," RevCycle Intelligence, *Practice Management News*, July 14, 2016. https://revcycleintelligence. com/news/understanding-the-basics-of-bundled-payments-in-healthcare. (Accessed on June 19, 2018.)

33. Vera Gruessner, "CMS Issues Bundled Payment Models for Cardiac, Orthopedic Care," HealthPayer Intelligence, Value-Based Care News, December 22, 2016. https:// healthpayerintelligence.com/news/cms-issues-bundled-payment-models-for-cardiac-orthopedic-care. (Accessed on June 19, 2018.)

34. Vera Gruessner, "Private Payers Follow CMS Lead, Adopt Value-Based Care Payment," HealthPayer Intelligence, *Value-Based Care News*, October 17, 2016. https://healthpayerintelligence. com/news/private-payers-follow-cms-lead-adopt-value-based-care-payment. (Accessed on June 19, 2018.)

35. This is consistent with the overall approach to health services favored by many Republicans in Congress and the White House. See Erin Dietsche, "CMS Cancels Mandatory Hip Fracture and Cardiac Bundled Payment Models," MedCity News, December 1, 2017. https://medcitynews.com/2017/12/ cms-bundled-payment-models/. (Accessed on June 19, 2018.)

Chapter 11

Concluding Observations

In the preceding chapters, nine factors have been identified that individually and collectively create a level of complexity for the health care industry that sets it apart from every other industry in our country's economy. In the end, complexity has many implications:

- Makes it more difficult to understand how the industry "works"
- Leads to a lack of clarity regarding overall goals and direction
- Provides opportunities for politicians, administrators, clinicians and patients to hold very different understandings about "cause and effect"
- Presents significant challenges on the ability to transfer many common business practices to health care
- Slows the adoption of new technologies, techniques, processes and policies
- Permits ideology to drive both internal and external decision-making, leading to very different (and often strongly held) views about who should have access to health care services and who should pay for them

■ Creates high levels of frustration among politicians seeking to lower costs, administrators seeking to manage complex institutions and clinicians and patients looking for better outcomes

Over the years, information technology (IT) investments have gradually impacted every aspect of health care, while also changing (much more consistently) virtually every industry in America, and much of the world as well. However, the costs and benefits of IT investments that seem so clear in driving higher productivity, the development of better products, and lower costs in other industries, have been much less successful in health care. Complexity has its consequences, even with IT.

IT investments in many cases are a double-edged sword—computerized factories can enable some workers to be more productive while at the same time putting others out of the work; electronic documents can facilitate the sharing of data while at the same time exposing that data to risks of inappropriate access and disclosure; computer capabilities used well in structured production environments are much less successful when attempts are made to transfer those capabilities to less structured environments (such as clinical workflows).

Here is a brief summary of the complexity challenges discussed in the preceding chapters:

■ Health care, as a "services-based" business, doesn't facilitate the specific measurement methodologies common to "product-based" businesses.
■ Physicians play a unique role in health care with few similarities to roles in other industries.
■ Patients as consumers/customers often do not understand the specifics of their own health nor of the health care services they receive.

- There are significant challenges to measuring the return on IT investments and the quality of health care services that are provided in the health care industry.
- The field of medicine generally is becoming more complex, especially with the onset of genomic medicine.
- Standards for the patient data that is collected and stored have been very difficult to establish and use.
- Health care data has unique challenges related to the privacy and security mandates of the federal government that apply specifically to the health care industry.
- The complexity of health care opens the door to political maneuvering, both at the national level and within individual provider organizations.
- Standard economic market mechanisms, including the allocation of resources and the setting of prices, appear not to work well in the health care industry, especially with much of the payment for health care services coming from third parties who are not directly involved in the buyer/seller transaction.

A recent comment on a health care blog noted the challenges of the health care industry, and indirectly, the extraordinary complexity of this industry:

- Health care is a profession, actually many of them with independent training and licensing requirements.
- Health care is a utility, regulated for access and performance. There are barriers to entry, barriers to change.
- The industry is both capital intensive and labor intensive—new technologies are often additive and seldom substitute for labor.
- Health care requires scale, yet each locality expects its own full-service medical complement and 24/7 institution.
- The physician supply is limited (residency slots and increasingly, immigration policy) and the fiefdoms that are

the medical specialties are protected by tradition, trade groups, and government policy.

■ Health care actors (providers, insurers, governments) are masters at skewing the risk to their own advantage (payer mix, provider licensing, underwriting).

■ Insiders often have their own myopia about how the industry operates.

■ Outsiders have been defeated before.

■ Approach with humility and be prepared for a fight.[1]

It seems fitting to conclude this discussion with the same quote used at the beginning:

I have to tell you, it's an unbelievable complex subject ... nobody knew that health care could be so complicated.[2]

Now *you* know!

Notes

1. http://www.paulkeckley.com/the-keckley-report/2018/2/5/is-the-amazon-jp-morgan-berkshire-hathaway-venture-armaged-don-for-healthcare-as-we-know-it?rq=amazon%20. (Accessed on June 19, 2018.) The sentences have been separated for emphasis. This comment was posted by Thomas O'Brien to a blog written by Paul Keckley (www.paulkeckley.com). The comment was made in response to Paul Keckley's observations about the announcement by Amazon, Berkshire Hathaway, and JP Morgan of a coordinated effort to reduce their spending on the healthcare of their employees. For more discussion about the corporate efforts, see https://www.businesswire.com/news/home/20180130005676/en/Amazon-Berkshire-Hathaway-JPMorgan-Chase-partner-U.S. (Accessed on June 19, 2018.)
2. President Donald Trump, televised press conference, February 27, 2017. https://www.youtube.com/watch?v=NXFr6_cJJTc. (Accessed on June 26, 2018.)

Index